Emergency Preparedness
Bioterrorism and Beyond

Elaine R. Rubin
Marian Osterweis
Lisa M. Lindeman
Editors

Association of Academic Health Centers
Washington, DC

The Association of Academic Health Centers (AHC) is a national nonprofit organization dedicated to improving the health of the people by advancing the leadership of academic health centers in health professions education, biomedical and health services research, and health care delivery.

The views expressed in this book are those of its authors and do not necessarily represent the views of the Board of Directors of the Association of Academic Health Centers or the membership at large.

Library of Congress Cataloging-in-Publication Data
Emergency preparedness: bioterrorism and beyond/Elaine R. Rubin, Marian Osterweis, Lisa M. Lindeman.
　　　　p.　　cm.
Includes biographical references (p.).
ISBN 1-879-694-22-0
1. Bioterrorism.　2. Civil defense—United States.
I. Rubin, Elaine R.
II. Osterweis, Marian.　III. Lindeman, Lisa M.
RA645.5 .E496 2002
363.34'97—dc21　　　　　　　　　　　2002026200

Available from:
Association of Academic Health Centers
1400 Sixteenth Street, NW
Suite 720
Washington, DC 20036

Voice 202/265-9600
Fax 202/265-7514
www.ahcnet.org

Price: $25.00

Design by Fletcher Design, Inc., Washington, DC
Text editing by SSR Incorporated, Washington, DC

Contents

Contributors

C. Ross Anthony, PhD, is interim director, Center for Domestic and International Health Security, RAND Corporation.

Mark Crockett, MD, is president, IBEX Healthdata Systems, Inc.

Maggie Fox is health and science correspondent, Reuters News Service.

Donald A. Henderson, MD, MPH, is director, Office of Public Health Preparedness, U.S. Department of Health and Human Services.

Robert E. Hunter, PhD, is senior advisor, RAND Corporation, and former U.S. ambassador to NATO.

Lisa M. Lindeman is program associate, Association of Academic Health Centers.

Henri R. Manasse Jr., PhD, ScD, is executive vice president and CEO, American Society of Health-System Pharmacists.

Martin Michaelson, JD, is partner, Hogan & Hartson.

Marian Osterweis, PhD, is executive vice president and director, Division of Global Health, Association of Academic Health Centers.

Betty Pfefferbaum, MD, JD, is professor and chairman, Department of Psychiatry and Behavioral Sciences, University of Oklahoma Health Sciences Center.

Elaine R. Rubin, PhD, is vice president for program, Association of Academic Health Centers.

Eve Slater, MD, is assistant secretary for health, U.S. Department of Health and Human Services.

Leonard S. Spector, JD, is deputy director, Center for Nonproliferation Studies, Monterey Institute of International Studies.

Lew Stringer Jr., MD, is medical director, North Carolina Division of Emergency Management, and supervisory medical officer, National Disaster Medical System.

Jonathan B. Tucker, PhD, is director, Chemical and Biological Weapons Nonproliferation Program, Monterey Institute of International Studies.

James A. Zimble, MD, is president, Uniformed Services University of the Health Sciences.

Preface

E mergency preparedness, a matter of urgent national policy in today's new world, is shifting agendas and creating new programs in both private organizations and public agencies. Nationally, September 11 has forced a reappraisal of domestic and foreign policy agendas that affect not only the United States but also the world. At Federal and local and state levels, where most of the immediate response to a disaster will take place, the events of September 11 have galvanized health care leaders and major institutions to reassess the broad spectrum of emergency preparedness, ranging from natural disasters to bombing, biological, air, and nuclear attacks.

Academic health centers are at the nexus of response and preparedness. Emergency preparedness is, in a sense, an underpinning of their basic missions—education, research, and service—and September 11 was a tragic reminder of their expansive, evolving roles and responsibilities in public health systems at every level. Their professors, researchers, and health professionals are at the core of health care services and biomedical research enterprises throughout the nation.

Academic health center professionals are instrumental in developing strategies, policies, and practices for the full range of emergency preparedness issues from infectious disease agents to interdisciplinary training programs. Substantial numbers of academic health center personnel are trainers, first-responders, and caregivers who have long been on the front line of the nation's defense in a multitude of crises, regardless of origin. And because their institutions are significant players in local, state, and regional economies, their leaders are increasingly being recognized for their roles in developing public policy.

This book compiles a set of papers highlighting emergency preparedness issues, strategies, policies, and practices that are changing the American landscape since September 11. In so doing, they draw attention to a host of complex, interrelated areas, including health care services, the development and access to biologics, immigration, the impact on education, and research capacity. Responding to powerful new forces and threats, they debate and analyze such issues as local versus regional response mechanisms, the nature of information dissemination in times of crisis, and the risks and benefits of preparedness.

Leonard Spector, a leading authority on international security and nuclear proliferation, opens the discussion with a new socioeconomic political framework against which he highlights how the agendas for national security, international cooperation, the global economy, university roles and responsibilities, and public expectations—and threats—must be analyzed. Dr. Tucker offers his perspective from the viewpoint of an expert in biologics, on the nation's preparedness for bioterrorism, the characteristics of biological terrorists, and ways to reduce the risks associated with bioterrorism.

Dr. Henderson, who led the establishment of the Office of Homeland Security, addresses the government's role and the opportunities and challenges of improving public health in the post-September 11 world. Dr. Slater, with her expertise in health, pharmaceuticals, and public policy, comments on the larger policy agenda for the U.S. Department of Health and Human Services and how emergency preparedness fits with current public concerns for access to health care services and traditional HHS priorities.

Dr. Manasse, CEO of the American Society of Health-System Pharmacists, analyzes critical issues of pharmaceutical supply and demand in the event of a national emergency. He notes that academic health centers "provide community leadership regarding drug information . . . that can serve as an ethical nexus for a public debate on unanswerable questions" related to information dissemination and individual and collective risk. Dr. Stringer delineates the importance of state and local response networks, offering insights drawn from his work with city and state disaster officials, on leadership and management issues for institutional and community leaders.

Dr. Zimble, CEO of the nation's military academic health center, presents models for education and practice based on experiences and traditions from military medicine. Putting their papers together in one chapter, Ambassador Hunter and Dr. Anthony look at work underway at RAND's Center for Domestic and International Health Security. Hunter, the former

U.S. Ambassador to NATO, provides insight on how the nature of security has changed and the implications of such change for health in a new paradigm. Anthony, an expert in global health and public policy, carries on the discussion of how health affects important variables related to the goals of foreign policy, concluding with some observations about special roles for academic health centers.

As a lawyer well-versed in higher education issues, Martin Michaelson explores a broad spectrum of legal, ethical, and management concerns currently challenging and affecting higher education in the aftermath of September 11. Maggie Fox, a reporter who covers health and science matters, believes that the government undervalues people's ability to handle bad news sensibly; she describes how academic health centers can work with the press to disseminate timely and accurate information. Drawing on survivors' experiences after the Oklahoma City bombing, Dr. Pfefferbaum, a psychiatrist, examines new findings on the psychological impact of terrorism on those left behind, with special reference to children. Finally, Dr. Crockett, a physician with special knowledge of electronic data-collection in emergency rooms, describes how an academic health center can expand an existing data-collection system into a network for public health surveillance; it is undoubtedly a forerunner of other technologies that will be mustered in the cause of preparedness.

This book is a unique addition to the emerging literature about September 11, for it is the first since that day of disaster to focus on the broad spectrum of emergency preparedness, particularly in academe. The importance of preparedness and the need for multiple capacities at a variety of sites emphasizes the need to fully integrate health and higher education systems into surveillance and delivery strategies and operations.

We are pleased to be able to publish these papers and present these perspectives to a wider audience. We wish to thank The Robert Wood Johnson Foundation for its generous support for the publication and dissemination of this work. We also express our appreciation for the editorial assistance provided by Shirley Sirota Rosenberg of SSR, Incorporated, and the graphic design skill of Richard Fletcher of Fletcher Design.

ERR

MO

LL

Chapter One

A New Geopolitical Landscape

Leonard S. Spector, JD

T he tragedy of September 11 and what next transpired—the anthrax letters and other related developments—are now beginning to intersect the world of international security and the world of the health sciences. As this paper shows, the health sciences are now on the front line of the nation's defense, and the academic health centers have an enormously important role to play in the process.

For many decades, academic health centers have been working on the conquest of disease, reducing infant mortality, extending life expectancy, advocating for expanded health care coverage, and decoding the human genome. Although the progress in the health sciences has not been uniformly perfect, when people think of the health professions and the health sciences, they tend to see progress. On the other hand, during the past decade, the world has been gradually going from being a dangerous but manageable world to one where shifting and amorphous threats are making it more dangerous every year. In international security, the tools to deal with these challenges have been embedded in our culture, but now seem to have only marginal utility. Although the field of international security has experienced a number of successes, when people think of international security, they sense growing danger, anxiety, pessimism, uncertainty, insecurity, and an erosion of confidence.

International Security in the Early 1990s

Former CIA Director James Woolsey testified in the early 1990s on the reality of the new world order. Speaking of the Soviet Union, he said, "We've slain a large dragon, but now we live in a jungle filled with a bewildering variety of poisonous snakes." The snakes that Director Woolsey alluded to are a good deal more numerous and venomous than he could have imagined.

People in the field of international security were then focused on weapons of mass destruction (WMDs). They were concentrating on ensuring stability and continuity within the Soviet nuclear arsenal because responsibility for the nuclear arsenal had spread. Four countries, not just one, now had some of those assets—Russia, Belarus, Kazakhstan, and Ukraine. The United States launched heavy diplomatic efforts to try to denuclearize Belarus, Kazakhstan, and Ukraine and other elements of the Soviet nuclear weapons legacy. We were securing that program against leakage to other countries, especially to rogue nations. We were also concerned about WMDs elsewhere.

Nuclear nonproliferation efforts were targeted to dismantling Saddam Hussein's nuclear capabilities when, after the Gulf War, U.N. inspections revealed the surprisingly advanced status of his nuclear program. The United States was also probing North Korea's nuclear past. North Korea was finally permitting some international inspectors into the country, who found that North Korea had produced plutonium, the material used in nuclear weapons. North Korea said they were using only in tiny quantities. Later, inspectors would discover that North Korea had enough plutonium to produce one or two nuclear devices.

Also at that time, inspectors were confirming South Africa's denuclearization and its renunciation of nuclear weapons. With the end of the Soviet threat in southern Africa, the white minority government realized it did not need nuclear weapons anymore. As part of its overall transition into a more modern and democratic existence, South Africa decided to eliminate them. The United States was fostering that program, and inspectors were going in to determine that the nuclear weapon program had been completely shut down.

At the same time, chemical and biological weapons and missile capabilities were known to be a threat in other countries, although the threat seemed manageable. Saddam Hussein had biological and chemical weapons during the Gulf War, but did not use them. It appeared that he may have been deterred by the veiled threat of nuclear retaliation by the United States or Israel.

The missile threat also seemed to be manageable. With the exception of Iraq, where inspectors were present and destroying missiles, the most that other countries of concern could do was fire a short-range scud at a neighboring country. Iran might have been able to fire a scud into Iraq, or North Korea into South Korea, but not farther than that.

What did the map of dangers from weapons of mass destruction look like? (In fact, there actually was a map to plot out who was doing what, and where.) We had fairly good information about the status of the WMD programs. We also knew that around each country was a penumbra where each country could strike its neighbors with short-range missiles.

One area, however, was becoming increasingly foggy. What was going to happen with the Soviet nuclear capabilities and nuclear materials and their biological and chemical capabilities? Would they leak out? The United States believed that, if they did leak, they would do so to national capitals such as Pyongyang, Tripoli, Baghdad, and Tehran, and not to nonstate types of organizations. Thus, ten years ago, we thought we knew how to deal with such evolving threats.

Traditional Ways of Dealing with Threats

The United Nations and the United States had spent decades dealing with these kinds of challenges. The United States had nuclear deterrents and a powerful military. We had a good treaty, the Strategic Arms Reduction Treaty (START 1), banning nuclear weapons, which most countries had joined and, by and large, they were keeping the lid on their missile programs and reporting where this was not being done. For countries who had not signed the treaty, the treaty was still a useful tool for galvanizing international responses. In 1992, the Conference on Disarmament at Geneva was about to complete the Convention on the Prohibition of the Development, Production, Stockpiling, and Use of Chemical Weapons and on their Destruction, the second big prohibitory treaty. Countries had also signed the Convention on the Prohibition of the Development, Production and Stockpiling of Bacteriological (Biological) and Toxin Weapons and on Their Destruction. However, no one knew how weak its provisions would be until later.

The United Nations had inspection arrangements, especially in Iraq and other countries suspected of sponsoring programs to build weapons of mass destruction. The United States had powerful export controls that were rather good at restricting the sales of dangerous technologies. (Nuclear technology is hard to mask; only a few companies in the world produce nuclear technology, and it has very limited uses.)

The United States also had diplomacy: jawboning, arm-twisting, sanctions, and incentives. All told, we had a sense that we could stay on top of things.

New Tools to Deal with New Threats

Obviously, the picture has changed dramatically. In some ways, we have developed a number of new tools, some of which have been proven to be very effective. Other new tools to deal with emerging dangers are just unfolding.

Cooperative Threat Reduction

In 1991, to manage the leakage of material for weapons of mass destruction out of the former Soviet Union, the United States developed a rather revolutionary approach, cooperative threat reduction (CTR). Sponsored by Senators Sam Nunn (D-Ga.) and Richard Lugar (R-Ind.), the CTR and non-proliferation programs provided funds to Russia to help dismantle the nuclear weapons systems that needed to be destroyed under the START 1 treaty. CTR also helped create jobs at nuclear and biological weapons sites to keep scientists in place so they would not drift off to countries of concern. CTR provided hundreds of millions of dollars to physically secure nuclear materials, and is still doing that today.

A CTR program at the Department of Energy (DoE) provided foreign aid to Belarus, Kazakhstan, and Ukraine and a promise of linkage to the United States. The program sought to counter Russian influence as a way of inducing these countries to give up their nuclear weapons. By 1996, all had done so. The last weapons went back to Russia in 1996, creating just one nuclear-successor state to the former Soviet Union.

Counter-Proliferation Programs

In 1994, DoE, the Department of Defense (DoD), and U.S. intelligence agencies created a counter-proliferation program as part of the 1994 National

Defense Authorization Act (NDAA). The counter-proliferation program was to assess military capabilities and their possible use for dealing with weapons of mass destruction. The purpose was to protect U.S. forces against chemical and biological weapon attack in the field and to develop short-range defenses against missiles such as the scud. The program also looked for ways to destroy enemy stockpiles of weapons of mass destruction in wartime.

That same year, the government struck a unique deal with North Korea. North Korea would freeze the dangerous parts of its nuclear program (which they did) in return for a promise that the United States would supply fewer proliferation-prone nuclear power plants of the kind that we have and that we could control quite well. The deal has been controversial, but it has been an effective way to keep the lid on this particular problem.

Emerging Threats

Just as the United States was beginning to enjoy a degree of success in preventing nuclear proliferation and feeling a sense of accomplishment in adapting to a new environment, three major new threats unfolded. The first was, of course, the substantial growth in the spread of missile capabilities. By 1992, Iran, North Korea, India, and Pakistan had all acquired missile systems capable of reaching some distance. Iran can now reach Israel. North Korea can now reach Japan, and has also tested a missile, the Taep'o-dong 1 (TD-1), which has flown over Japan. If adapted and modernized, it could eventually reach the United States. North Korea says that the missile is a vehicle for launching satellites, but everyone in the business knows that these kinds of systems can be adapted to deliver warheads into orbit.

The United States does not feel directly threatened by India and Pakistan's nuclear capabilities. However, the fact that they now can have intermediate-range missiles has contributed to the fear of a confrontation in that part of the world could evolve into a nuclear exchange. Pakistan can strike deep into India, and India can transport its missiles almost anywhere in its own country and hit Pakistan, leaving no doubt that missiles with a growing capability are spreading and will probably continue to spread to additional nations.

To address the new missile threats, the Clinton Administration, somewhat reluctantly, and now the Bush Administration, quite enthusiastically, moved to develop missile defenses against these longer-range systems.

These defense systems remain many years away—at least those systems for defending against the very long-range systems. In the meantime, the United States is going to have to rely on the traditional tools—deterrents and diplomacy—to try to contain this challenge.

Another disturbing development during the past ten years has been the arrival of the biological weapons threat. Until recently and certainly during the Cold War, it was in the background; however, this threat is now here with a vengeance. In 1992, Ken Alibek defected from the Soviet Union. Alibek, who had led part of the USSR biological weapons establishment there, supplied many new details about what the Russians were doing. Alibek's book, Biohazard: The Chilling True Story of the Largest Covert Biological Weapons Program in the World-Told from Inside by the Man Who Ran It, was explicit. At that time, the Russians were developing a program to produce hundreds of tons of disease agent propelled by sophisticated delivery systems. The program was horrifying, probably even more so for people in the health professions than for a person working on the outside. One of the most disturbing, and perhaps despicable, elements of the program was that as the international community was celebrating the end of smallpox as a naturally occurring disease, the Russians were deliberately surging up to use smallpox as a weapon of mass destruction. They knew that the population against which they might use this disease was now going to be highly vulnerable because of the end of the mass innoculation campaigns.

Other elements of the program included the development of antibiotic-resistant anthrax and research to create hybrids that would combine the lethality of certain illnesses with the contagiousness of others. Although Boris Yeltsin ordered the program shut down in 1992, the U.S. government believes that capabilities continue to exist and research on offensive biological weapons may still be going on at certain locations.

As the United States was absorbing all of Alibek's information, Saddam Hussein's son-in-law, Hussein Kamal, defected as well. He brought with him detailed information about the Iraqi biological weapons program. The government knew the program existed but did not have details. After Kamal defected and the United States learned what he had to say, we sent inspectors back in to Iraq; however, there was still a question about whether the full program had been unearthed.

The Iraqi program was not on the same scale as the Russian program, so it did not pose the same style of threat. But they had weaponized anthrax and several other bugs, at least to a certain level of sophistication. In 1998, U.N. inspectors were withdrawn from Iraq because Iraq no longer permitted them access to nuclear, biological, or any other sites. Whatever Saddam Hussein was working on in 1991, he was almost certainly working on behind the scenes when the U.N. inspectors were present. He is now most definitely working assiduously to upgrade this capability. Knowing how much capability is out there, and how seriously some countries take biological weapons as a military instrument, is certainly disturbing.

By the mid-1990s, weapons of mass destruction were spreading to an entirely new type of actor: organizations straight out of a James Bond movie. (The villains in the James Bond movies are always these large-scale, international, nonstate organizations with virtually unlimited funds, considerable technical resources, a safe home base, and, not unusually, a megalomaniacal leader out to destroy the world.) One such organization was the Japanese religious cult, Aum Shinrikyo, a group that came to prominence in 1995 when it released the nerve gas sarin in the Tokyo subways. Their attack killed 12 people, injured 5,000 others, and frightened thousands. What was not well publicized at the time was that, previously, Aum Shinrikyo had attempted numerous times to use germ warfare to sow chaos and cause large numbers of casualties. They had tried to disperse anthrax and botulinum toxin on several occasions but, as far as we know, without result. It is unclear why the botulinum toxin may have failed. It appears that in our country, the anthrax attack failed because the group had a strain that may not have been sufficiently virulent. Nevertheless, biological weapons were part of Aum Shinrikyo's world as well, and they worked assiduously to try to make sarin a success.

The attacks of September 11, and the subsequent mailing of the anthrax letters have made clear that two trends—the emergence of biological weapons and the emergence of globalized nonstate actors—are not passing phenomena. They are enduring features of the international security landscape. Fortunately, there appears to be no direct link between Al Qaeda and the anthrax letters. Al Qaeda seems to have made little progress in developing weapons of mass destruction, notwithstanding the finding of the anthrax lab near Kandahar. But the anthrax letters with their high quality, weaponized agent and the known interest of Al Qaeda in weapons of mass destruction certainly leaves no doubt in my mind as to as to where we are heading.

State Actors

Compounding the dangers of anthrax and nonstate actors are the state actors and their ways of making mischief. A number of the states sponsoring terrorism, especially Iran, Iraq, and North Korea, are the very countries thought to possess or to be developing biological weapons.

Moreover, there is a connection between the radical elements of Iran and radical elements of the Palestinian community. Both money and conventional arms being transferred. Some of the conventional arms are deliberately more destructive, powerful explosives to replace the homemade explosives used by the Palestinian radicals. One has to wonder: What might be in store for the future? Will a crude form of anthrax that is not so highly weaponized and traceable to a national government find its way from Iran or Iraq into the hands of radical groups working in the Middle East? The Bush Administration has been talking about the possibility that Saddam Hussein is assisting terrorist organizations in this way. Although, to date there is no evidence that such assistance has occurred, it is a possibility.

The United States also has to realize that potentially hostile countries observed what happened on September 11, reinforcing for them a way to hurt us with the so-called asymmetric approach. The United States can surge aircraft carriers and bombers into their regions, but the others are unable to retaliate in the same way because they do not have the same equipment. However, they have observed how painful and devastating lesser attacks can be to the United States, and certainly can imagine launching much more potent attacks than in the past.

A national intelligence estimate released in January 2002 looked at the missile threat to the United States through 2015. (This estimate came from the Central Intelligence Agency (CIA) during a Republican Administration known to support missile defenses.) It read, in part, as follows:

> Everyone in the field of international security anticipated that this document would overstate the missile threat to the United States and minimize, or not even mention, the possibility of nonmissile capabilities that might be used against us. Not only was the characterization of the missile threat balanced, but a prominent section of the report discussed the nonmissile threat, that is, the threat from countries using the modalities of terrorists against us. Nonmissile WMD threats (weapons of mass destruction threats) to the United States: although non-missile means of delivering WMD do not provide the same pres-

tige or degree of deterrence or coercive diplomacy associated with an ICBM, an intercontinental [ballistic] missile, such options are of significant concern. Countries or non-state actors could pursue non-missile delivery options, most of which are less expensive than developing and producing ICBMs, most of which can be covertly developed and employed and mask the source of the weapon being used in an attempt to evade retaliation. Most non-weapons systems would probably be more reliable than ICBMs that have not completed rigorous testing and validation programs. Most non-missile delivery options would probably be more accurate than emerging ICBMs for the next 15 years, and probably would be more effective for disseminating biological weapons agents than a ballistic missile. And of course, most all of them, by definition would avoid missile defenses.

Clearly, the intelligence community is thinking about these threats and anticipating that the other side is doing so, as well.

New Responses to New Threats

In this environment, how should we address the new threats ? The traditional tools of deterrence and diplomacy and the more modern tools such as cooperative threat reduction all have a role to play, but none of them will work alone. Even taken together, they may not be up to the task.

Deterrence through the threat of retaliation may not deter an amorphous organization with apocalyptic goals or one whose members anticipate martyrdom or have no homeland, no population, and no physical assets that they cherish and want to protect against retaliation. They are far less likely than states to be deterred by retaliation for engaging in acts of mass violence. The U.S. nuclear arsenal, the bulwark of the nation's defense since the end of World War II, has no role to play in addressing threats from this particular quarter. Deterrence through the threat of retaliation is also problematic. This is because in the event of a biological weapon attack, including one undertaken by a state, we may not know who did it or how or where to retaliate. The United States still has not identified the perpetrators of the anthrax terrorism.

Treaties will offer some indirect help, but may not be effective for dealing with nonstate actors operating in lawless states. Although the treaties include criminal statutes to stop individuals from developing biological and chemical weapons, in some states, such as Somalia, these statutes just do not apply.

In law-abiding countries like Japan and others that have effective law enforcement, the biological weapons threat is so slippery that it is difficult to get one's hands around it . The equipment and many of the agents are used widely for commercial purposes. The same is true for export controls; adapting them effectively to the biological weapons area is very difficult.

Because the United States is not dealing with states, it is hard to imagine how our government could have a diplomatic exchange with Al Qaeda and work out a deal like the one with North Korea. Cooperative threat reduction certainly has a role to play, but cannot solve the problem alone. Although missile defenses also have a role to play, such defenses may not be effective for some of these.

Thus far, the United States has been adding significant new dimensions to what Americans traditionally think of as the national defense . In particular, we are adding counter-terorrism. Counterterrorism was never part of our national defense until now; it was always a stand-alone area for defending against a specialized threat. Homeland security is now a major new part of the nation's armamentarium. If the United States cannot deter these organizations from striking with WMDs or has difficulty controlling the means for producing some of these weapons, we need to take action against the groups themselves. In the event of failure, we must be able to defend ourselves against the attack when it comes.

Counter-terrorism seeks to disrupt terrorist organizations before they can grow and develop to the point where they can get some of these advanced weapons. It involves denying the terrorists sanctuary and blocking their funding. These actions are part of the war on terrorism, and the United States is obviously making every effort in this direction. Counterterrorism involves military force, but military forces adapted to a new mission, with intelligence and law enforcement integrated to address the nonstate threat.

Homeland security is a radical new element in the nation's defense planning. The government has not looked at homeland security since the 1950s. Civil defense was somewhat discredited as a way of providing protection against a massive Soviet attack. Because the nation had no other threat in the intervening years , homeland security ceased to be a significant part of the national defense. After the Soviet Union collapsed, the government began to look more closely at protecting elements of our domestic critical infrastructure. This approach changed substantially after September 11.

The big change occurred at nuclear power plants. The Nuclear Regulatory Commission (NRC) had a regulation that the government did not need to protect nuclear power plants against enemies of the United States. The regulation mentioned protection against terrorists, but not against enemies of the United States with substantial military capability. In November 2001, when the Office of Homeland Security was chartered, one leading element of its charter was to marshal all resources of Federal, state, and local governments, and the private sector to protect nuclear power plants and other nuclear assets against terrorist organizations of international dimensions.

Academic Health Centers and Homeland Security

Until ten years ago, the role of the health sciences in international security was modest, focused on dealing with military threats or casualties suffered in the Gulf War, preparing vaccines, vaccinating the armed forces against anthrax, and preparing antidotes to nerve gas, et cetera. The military was also preparing specialized medical units and facilities to deal with casualties they feared might occur. Homeland security has now become the area in which academic health centers will be most active, with the government looking to the health sciences and health professionals to help meet the challenge of mass terrorism, especially from biological weapons. Academic health centers, for example, will be working to develop and stockpile vaccines and therapeutics to blunt the impact of a biological weapons attack and providing disease- monitoring capabilities to track and manage biological weapons attacks. They will prepare emergency plans, deal with the consequences of an attack, and manage what may be thousands of casualties at multiple locations. Academic health centers will also be training new professionals in building infrastructure and engaging in advanced coordination so that the nation can marshal all its resources effectively when necessary.

In the long term, the role of academic health centers may be even more central. Champions of missile defense believe that the United States could block intercontinental missiles from many of the developing countries that we worry about. We might reinforce the nation's military strength to such a degree that adversaries will not only be deterred from launching missiles at us, but feel it is not worth the effort and investment to develop the missiles in the first place. A comparable scenario may be possible in the health field as academic health centers dig in and work away at some of the biological weapons threats. If we had effective vaccines or therapeutics for all the traditional biological weapons agents, we could, in a sense, transform at least a part of the problem. Although new bugs will be created, and methods will need to be developed for dealing with them, vaccines and therapies for the traditional microbes will change the dynamics and, at least briefly, give the United States the upper hand.

Conclusion

Just as the map of dangers from weapons of mass destruction no longer defines geographic boundaries, so have the front lines in the battlefield shifted to include both distant lands and communities in the United States. For the foreseeable future, Americans will be facing a spectrum of threats never confronted before. To meet these threats, we have to work together to mount a comprehensive, full-spectrum, and all-points-of-the-compass response. Preventive tools can only accomplish part of the mission. Academic health center laboratories, classrooms, and hospitals must be on the forward edge of battle as the nation tries to handle the struggle ahead.

Chapter Two

Assessing the Threat of Bioterrorism

Jonathan B. Tucker, PhD

Bioterrorism, once a largely hypothetical threat, now poses a clear and present danger to U.S. national security. In the autumn of 2001, a series of letters containing a total of about ten grams of powdered anthrax spores caused five deaths and several illnesses, and terrified millions of Americans. The anthrax letter attacks also had a disproportionate economic impact resulting in the widespread contamination of U.S. Post Offices and Federal buildings, closing them for months, and requiring the irradiation of government mail. All told, the ripple effects of the anthrax letters caused billions of dollars in damage.

The anthrax letters also had a demonstration effect: Other terrorists witnessed the far-reaching consequences of even a limited release of a weaponized biological agent and may have been inspired to replicate or even surpass it. Today, a large-scale attack on the United States with a biological agent remains a frightening possibility. In assessing the threat of bioterrorism, I first discuss the likely perpetrators and then the agents and dispersal techniques they might use.

Characteristics of Biological Terrorists

The groups and individuals most likely to engage in bioterrorism lie at the intersection of three sets: motivation, organizational structure, and technical capability (figure 1). Terrorist groups of greatest concern are motivated to inflict indiscriminate mass casualties and to engage in innovative and risky tactics. They have an organizational structure and internal control

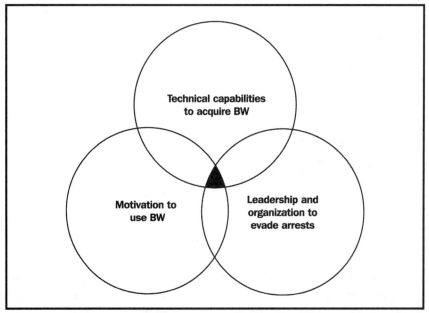

Figure 1. Characteristics of Terrorists Likely to Employ Biological Weapons

mechanisms that enable them to prevent penetration by government agents or defection by group members. Finally, they possess the technical capabilities and know-how to acquire, produce, and deliver biological weapons or to recruit scientific experts in these areas.

Historically, few terrorist groups have had the motivation, organization, and capability to conduct a successful bioterrorist attack. Some groups in the past have tried to acquire a biological warfare (BW) capability but have lacked the technical know-how to do so. Other groups have acquired a pathogen or toxin and been motivated to use it, but were penetrated by law enforcement or exposed by defectors before the attack could be carried out.

Is the number of groups capable of bioterrorism increasing? Long before the events of September 11 and the anthrax letter attacks, analysts began to observe ominous developments along all three dimensions of the bioterrorism threat. I will now briefly summarize these developments.

Motivation

Traditional terrorist organizations, such as the Irish Republican Army, have generally not tried to inflict indiscriminate mass casualties. Such groups have specific political aims, which they pursue by calibrating their use of violence to influence public opinion and apply pressure on government officials. It would be counterproductive for political terrorists to inflict too many casualties, for two reasons: (1) they have an outside constituency that would be alienated by indiscriminate attacks; and (2) resort to severe mayhem would provoke the government authorities to suppress the terrorists so aggressively that they would be destroyed as a viable organization.

Over the past decade, however, a new breed of terrorists has come on the scene. In general, these groups are prepared to inflict indiscriminate casualties because they are driven less by specific political goals and more by vague, inchoate belief systems, political extremism, or religious fundamentalism (table 1).

Whereas most terrorist groups in the 1960s and 1970s were motivated either by left-wing ideology (Marxist-Leninist or Maoist) or by nationalist-separatist ambitions, the number of groups characterized primarily by religious beliefs began to increase in the 1980s. According to terrorism analyst Bruce Hoffman, in 1968 none of the eleven major terrorist organizations then active were religiously motivated, yet today nearly one-fourth can be classified as primarily religious. Such groups either promote extreme forms of the world's major religions or entirely "new" belief systems, usually in the form of cults.

Religiously motivated terrorists are more likely than politically motivated groups to resort to nonconventional weapons, for the following reasons:
- They may desire not just to make a symbolic point but to physically annihilate their enemies.
- They may view extreme violence as divinely sanctioned and the fulfillment of God's commandments.
- They are largely unaffected by public opinion because they act on behalf of their deity or guru and their coreligionists.
- They may subscribe to apocalyptic prophecy and actively seek to bring about the end of the world.

A second new type of terrorist organization is focused around a single issue such as abortion, animal rights, environmental protection, or genetic engineering. Members of such groups feel passionately about their chosen issue and are prepared to strike out violently against those who disagree with them. The Army of God, for example, is an extremist antiabortion

Table 1. Motivational Factors in Biological Terrorism

PARANOIA AND GRANDIOSITY
- Delusions of persecution and international conspiracy.
- Pretense by individuals or small group to represent a larger community.
- Intoxicating sense of power and superiority.

NO POLITICAL CONSTITUENCY WITHIN THE TARGETED AREA
- No concern about alienating the target country's public.
- Dehumanization of victims.
- Few limits on action or constraints on level of violence.

SMALL CELL OR FACTION OF LARGER GROUP
- Group, cult, or cell psychologically isolated from larger society.
- Splinter group containing most radical elements of larger group.
- Members prone to take greater risks.
- Hothouse effect of cult thinking, group dynamics.

CHARISMATIC LEADER INCLINED TOWARD VIOLENCE
- Culture of violence in the community of belief.
- Distorted set of ethics and moral boundaries.
- Exploitation by leader of a sense of grievance; tendency to respond with violence to the outside world.
- God-like role of leader with unquestioned authority.

DEFENSIVE AGGRESSION
- Perception that group is under siege from outside authorities.
- Stockpiling of weapons may result, creating a self-fulfilling prophecy.

OTHER FACTORS THAT MAKE BW USE MORE LIKELY
- Escalating pattern of violence.
- Willingness to engage in risky behavior.
- Technical and tactical innovation and experimentation.
- Mystical fascination with poisons and biblical plagues.

Source. Tucker, Jonathan B., ed. 2000. *Toxic Terror: Assessing Terrorist Use of Chemical and Biological Weapons.* Cambridge, MA: MIT Press.

group that has assassinated doctors who perform abortions and sent hundreds of anthrax hoax letters to family-planning clinics around the United States.

The 1990s also saw the rise of right-wing terrorism, including neo-Nazis and neo-Fascists in Europe and white supremacist and antigovernment (Patriot) organizations in the United States. The Patriot movement subscribes to a conspiratorial worldview in which the Federal government is in league with Jewish bankers and the United Nations to deprive ordinary Americans of their land and liberty. Patriot groups in rural areas often form armed militias that stockpile weapons and conduct training exercises in preparation for a future showdown with the Federal government or U.N. troops. Some, but not all, members of the Patriot movement belong to the Christian Identity church, a twisted form of Christianity that is virulently racist and anti-Semitic. Many believers in the Patriot and Christian Identity ideologies constitute what terrorism analyst Jerrold Post has called a "community of belief," linked through e-mail and Internet Web sites rather than direct interpersonal contact. Timothy McVeigh, the Oklahoma City bomber, was not a member of a formal Patriot organization but identified strongly with the antigovernment community of belief.

Recent years have also seen a change in terrorist methods. Most terrorists in the past have been conservative in their choice of weapons and tactics, innovating only when compelled to do so. During the 1970s, for example, most terrorist incidents involved airplane hijackings. Only when improvements in aviation security were introduced did terrorists develop new avenues of attack, such as hiding explosives in luggage. On September 11, however, the world saw a quantum leap in terrorist innovation: the use of passenger aircraft as flying bombs to attack large buildings. Shaped by a fanatical worldview, the Al Qaeda terrorists sought to kill as many Americans as possible while striking at symbolic targets of U.S. economic and military power. They also had no political constraint on their use of violence and were prepared to sacrifice their own lives in carrying out the attack.

Several pieces of evidence suggest that Al Qaeda is interested in acquiring biological weapons. The network's mastermind, Osama bin Laden, has stated openly that it is his "religious duty" to acquire weapons of mass destruction. Moreover, in March 2002, U.S. troops found an abandoned laboratory under construction near Kandahar, Afghanistan, where Al Qaeda apparently planned to develop BW agents. According to CIA Director George J. Tenet, "Documents recovered from Al Qaeda facilities in Afghanistan show that bin Laden was pursuing a sophisticated biological weapons research program." Although no evidence exists in the public domain that Al Qaeda has succeeded at producing BW agents or in recruiting former bioweapons scientists, the motivation to do so clearly exists.

Organization

Many terrorist groups in the past had a defined leadership and a rigid organizational structure. As a result, such organizations were vulnerable to penetration by law enforcement agents, defections by key members, or the arrest or killing of group leaders. In recent years, however, terrorists have modified their organizational structures to make them more resistant to penetration and defection.

First, a growing number of terrorist groups have adopted a decentralized structure in which small cells independently plan and implement attacks. The right-wing Patriot movement, which was extensively penetrated by the FBI during the 1970s and 1980s, responded by developing a new organizational strategy known as "leaderless resistance," in which local chapters of national Patriot or neo-Nazi organizations receive their marching orders from Web sites and other anonymous means, and carry out terrorist attacks on their own initiative. Such cells are not only more difficult for law enforcement officials to detect and penetrate, but the dynamics of small groups may make them more prone to extreme violence.

Second, unaffiliated terrorists have sometimes come together on a temporary basis to form an ad hoc group for the purpose of carrying out one or two attacks. For example, the terrorists who attempted to blow up the New York World Trade Center in 1993 had not worked together until Ramzi Yousef recruited them for this particular mission. If a terrorist group lacks a long-term history, it will be more difficult for law enforcement to identify them in advance and prevent them from acting.

Third, terrorism is no longer confined to particular countries and regions. A growing number of terrorist organizations today have bases, operatives, and targets in several countries. For example, Aum Shinrikyo, the Japanese doomsday cult, had operations in Russia and Australia as well as Japan. The transnational character of such groups enables them to shift operations rapidly from one country to another to evade law enforcement, and to purchase or smuggle weapons and equipment from multiple sources.

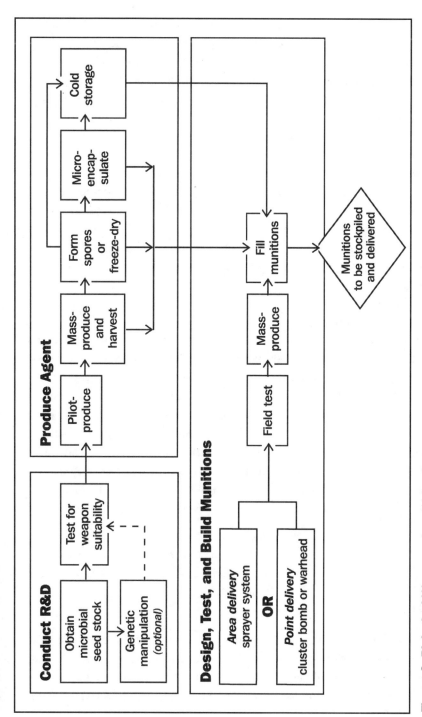

Figure 2. Biological Weapons Acquisition Process

Fourth, terrorist groups have increasingly sought to prevent internal defections by means of indoctrination, intimidation, and other means of social control. Aum Shinrikyo, for example, meted out severe punishment to dissidents and would-be defectors, including death.

The Al Qaeda network exemplifies the recent changes in the structure of terrorist organizations. It consists of a loosely coordinated web of cells that have a high degree of operational autonomy and are based in some forty countries in the Middle East, Africa, Asia, and North America. Al Qaeda operatives have a "virtual" headquarters and make use of advanced communications technologies such as encrypted e-mail messages and Web sites to coordinate their activities. Because of its highly decentralized network structure, Al Qaeda has no real "center of gravity" whose destruction would cause the organization to collapse, and procedures exist to reconstitute the leadership in the event key individuals such as Osama bin Laden are killed or arrested.

Technical Capability

With respect to the technical dimension of the bioterrorist threat, terrorists seeking to carry out a biological attack would have to overcome a series of challenging technical hurdles. Figure 2 illustrates the biological weapons acquisition process for a state-level program, but many of the same steps would apply to a subnational organization.

First, terrorists would have to obtain a microbial pathogen of sufficient virulence, either by culturing it from a natural source or by stealing or purchasing pathogenic strains from a research laboratory or a commercial culture collection. A partial list of classical BW threat agents includes:

- Anthrax
- Brucellosis
- Cholera
- Glanders
- Plague
- Tularemia

- Q fever
- Smallpox
- Venezuelan equine encephalitis
- Viral hemorrhagic fevers

- Botulism
- Staphylococcus enterotoxin B
- Ricin
- T-2 mycotoxin

These agents differ from one another in several characteristics. The infectious dose ranges from as little as 1 to 10 organisms (for Q fever) to 100 to 500 organisms (for inhalation anthrax). Incubation periods range from as little as one day (for botulism) to as much as fourteen days (for smallpox).

Duration and mortality vary substantially: Q fever is incapacitating but rarely fatal, whereas plague is nearly always fatal unless treated within twelve to twenty-four hours. Persistence of microorganisms in the environment also varies. Most microbial and toxin agents are fragile, particularly if exposed to sunlight, and die off rapidly when released into the air as a fine-particle aerosol. But spore-forming bacteria such as anthrax can survive for several hours as an airborne aerosol and for decades when buried in soil.

Whereas some BW agents are readily transmissible from person to person (such as smallpox or pneumonic plague), most are not. The advantage of a noncontagious agent is that it can be targeted at a specific population without the risk of spawning an epidemic that could boomerang against the attacking troops or friendly populations. During the 1950s and 1960s, when the United States had an offensive BW program, all of the agents it developed were noncontagious because that made them more controllable for military use.

Finally, BW agents differ in the availability of medical treatments and protective vaccines. Bacterial agents such as anthrax or tularemia generally respond to antibiotics if they are given early enough in the process of infection, but most viral diseases lack effective therapeutic interventions. Vaccines also vary in effectiveness and speed of action, and none are available for viral hemorrhagic fevers. Although an anthrax vaccine exists, it must be administered over a period of eighteen months prior to exposure to ensure a high level of protection. Smallpox vaccine is an exception to the rule because it can induce a protective level of immunity within several days. Indeed, the vaccine can prevent someone from contracting the disease or reduce its severity if administered up to four days after infection, but before the development of clinical symptoms.

The U.S. Centers for Disease Control and Prevention (CDC) has made an effort to categorize potential BW agents according to level of threat, using the following criteria:

- Public health impact, including transmissibility, morbidity, and mortality.
- Ease of production, dissemination potential as an aerosol, and environmental stability.
- Public perception of the disease, e.g., its psychological impact and ability to induce terror.
- Requirement for special preparation of the agent and potential for delivery as an airborne aerosol or by food or water contamination.

Table 2. Criteria and Weighting Used to Evaluate Potential Biological Threat Agents [from highest threat (+++) to lowest threat (0)]

Disease	Disease	Death	P-D[a]	p-p[b]	Public perception	Special preparation	Category
Smallpox	+	++	+	+++	+++	+++	A
Anthrax	++	+++	+++	0	+++	+++	A
Plague[c]	++	+++	++	++	++	+++	A
Botulism	++	+++	++	0	++	+++	A
Tularemia	++	++	++	0	+	+++	A
VHF[d]	++	+++	+	+	+++	++	A
VE[e]	++	+	+	0	++	++	B
Q fever	+	+	++	0	+	++	B
Brucellosis	+	+	++	0	+	++	B
Glanders	++	+++	++	0	0	++	B
Melioidosis	+	+	++	0	0	++	B
Psittacosis	+	+	++	0	0	+	B
Ricin toxin	++	++	++	0	0	++	B
Typhus	+	+	++	0	0	+	B
Cholera[f]	+	+	++	+/–	+++	+	B
Shigellosis[f]	+	+	++	+	+	+	B

[a] Potential for production and dissemination in quantities that affect a large population, based on availability, BSL requirements, most effective route of infection, and environmental stability.

[b] Person-to-person transmissibility.

[c] Pneumonic plague.

[d] Viral hemorrhagic fevers due to Filoviruses (Ebola, Marburg) or Arena viruses (e.g., Lassa, Machupo).

[e] Viral encephalitis.

[f] Examples of food- and waterborne diseases.

Source. Rota, Lisa D., Ali S. Kahn, Scott R. Lillibridge, Stephen M. Ostroff, and James M.Hughes. 2002. Public health assessment of potential biological terrorism agents. *Emerging Infectious Diseases* 8:2, February. <www.cdc.gov/ncidad/eid/vol8no2/01-0164.htm>

On this basis, the CDC has classified potential BW agents into three categories. Category A agents, which pose the greatest threat, include smallpox, anthrax, plague, botulism, tularemia, and viral hemorrhagic fevers (table 2). Smallpox would have the greatest public health impact if used as a terrorist weapon because it is readily transmissible from person to person and highly virulent (with the most lethal strains causing 30 to 40 percent mortality), and the fact that most Americans are susceptible to infection. Because the mandatory smallpox vaccination of children in the United States stopped in 1972 and the resulting immunity fades after about ten years, at least 80 percent of the U.S. population is now vulnerable to smallpox. The psychological impact of the disease is also great because the pustular skin rash is painful, disfiguring, and leaves survivors permanently scarred. Given the characteristics of the disease, a smallpox epidemic would be extremely demoralizing and disruptive.

Nevertheless, it is important not to exaggerate the threat of smallpox. The virus would be extremely difficult for terrorists to obtain because smallpox was eradicated as a natural disease in 1977 through a global vaccination campaign run by the World Health Organization (WHO); the last human case resulted from a laboratory accident in England the following year. Recent concern over the potential terrorist use of smallpox is due to the fact that samples of the live virus still exist in a few laboratories. In addition to WHO-approved repositories of smallpox virus in the United States and Russia, circumstantial evidence suggests that undeclared stocks may exist in Russia, Iraq, and North Korea. Also worrisome is the fact that during the 1980s, the Soviet military mass-produced the smallpox virus as a biological weapon for use against U.S. and Chinese cities in the event of World War III.

Once terrorists acquired a seed culture of a virulent pathogen, they would need to produce the agent in laboratory glassware or a small fermentation tank. They would then have to "weaponize" the agent, a process involving several steps. In the case of anthrax, the terrorists would first induce the bacteria to sporulate, a process in which the cells stop dividing and grow a tough outer coat that is resistant to the elements. Spore formation enables the bacteria to survive for long periods in a nutrient-poor environment by reverting to a state of suspended animation.

Terrorists could try to disseminate anthrax spores as a liquid slurry, but this physical form of the agent is extremely difficult to disseminate efficiently. Alternatively, they could attempt to freeze-dry or spray-dry the spores and then mill them into an extremely fine powder consisting of particles with microscopic dimensions. A fine powder of anthrax spores would be easier to disseminate in the form of an airborne aerosol: a neutrally buoyant suspension of invisibly small particles, similar to smoke, that would be inhaled by the target population.

Sophisticated terrorists might perform additional processing steps with dried anthrax spores to enhance their aerosolizability. These steps include adding desiccating chemicals to remove excess moisture and anti-agglomerants to neutralize the electrostatic charges on the particles and prevent them from clumping. These techniques far outstrip what Ph.D.-level microbiologists know, however; they are strictly military technologies that are generally classified and accessible only to bioweapons scientists.

Finally, the weaponized anthrax would have to be loaded into some type of delivery system, such as a spray tank mounted on a rooftop or a low-flying aircraft. Under optimal atmospheric conditions, such a device would generate a microbial aerosol that would be carried downwind by a gentle breeze to cover a wide area. Only particles ranging in size from one to five microns (thousandths of a millimeter) would lodge in the tiny air sacs of the victims' lungs. In the nutrient-rich environment of the lung, the anthrax spores would germinate and begin to multiply and cause infection.

In the case of a noncontagious BW agent such as anthrax bacteria, only individuals directly exposed to an infectious dose would be affected. Thus, to inflict mass casualties with anthrax, the terrorists would need a technologically advanced delivery system that could disseminate the agent as a concentrated aerosol over a wide area. An ordinary crop duster would not be suitable for this purpose because the spray nozzles would generate particles or droplets of agent too large to infect through the lungs. Instead, extensive modifications of the spray nozzles would be required. In the case of a contagious agent such as smallpox or pneumonic plague, however, terrorists could use a relatively low-tech aerosol sprayer to infect a small group of people, who would then spread the disease to others by secondary infection.

Some experts have speculated that suicide terrorists might deliberately infect themselves with a contagious disease such as smallpox or plague and then spread it to others. This means of dissemination would be possible only during the very brief period when the terrorists could transmit the disease through the air but were not visibly ill or incapacitated. Moreover, even suicide terrorists willing to die instantly in an explosion might think twice about suffering a slow, painful, and hideous death from smallpox.

Most of the steps involved in the acquisition, production, weaponization, and delivery of BW agents are technically challenging and have posed difficulties in the past for terrorist organizations. For example, Aum Shinrikyo sought to use biological weapons to inflict mass casualties, with the aim of fulfilling its leader's apocalyptic prophecies and seizing control of the Japanese government to impose a theocratic state. Flush with cash from a variety of legitimate and fraudulent businesses, the group recruited skilled microbiologists from Japanese universities. These individuals acquired seed cultures of the causative agents of anthrax and botulism, produced them in substantial quantities, and disseminated them in Tokyo on at least nine different occasions in 1990 and 1993. Fortunately for the residents of Tokyo, the Aum scientists had mistakenly selected nonvirulent strains of both *Clostridium botulinum*, the bacterium that produces botulinum toxin, and *Bacillus anthracis*, the bacterium that causes anthrax. Were it not for those technical errors, the biological attacks might have claimed a large number of victims.

More recently, the unknown perpetrator or perpetrators of the anthrax letter attacks succeeded in overcoming a series of major technical hurdles. Although the letters contained only a few grams of weaponized anthrax spores in the form of a finely ground powder, the material had been treated with chemical additives so that the spores became readily airborne and were inhaled by the victims. Of course, producing the kilograms of weaponized anthrax needed for a mass-casualty attack against an urban target would entail additional technical challenges and hazards.

Nevertheless, the methodical way in which the nineteen Al Qaeda terrorists planned the September 11 attacks over a period of years, learned how to fly sophisticated passenger aircraft, and eventually carried out the complex attack successfully is extremely troubling. This experience raises the possibility that if other Al Qaeda operatives were to apply the same systematic approach to the acquisition, weaponization, and large-scale delivery of biological agents, they might eventually overcome the technical barriers.

Sponsorship

Bioterrorists would not necessarily operate in isolation. At least in theory, they might be assisted by a state sponsor that possesses biological weapons and transfers them to the terrorists for a proxy attack on a third party. It is doubtful that even a rogue state like Iraq would be prepared to accept the loss of control, and the severe risk of attribution and retaliation, associated with this scenario. Nevertheless, state-sponsored bioterrorism might become somewhat more likely if Saddam Hussein was about to be removed from power or killed and, with nothing left to lose, decided to unleash smallpox or some other deadly BW agent as a final act of revenge against his enemies.

Also worrisome is the possibility that terrorists could recruit bioweapons experts formerly employed by a state-level BW program. The problem of "brain drain" is particularly serious in the states of the former Soviet Union, including Russia, Kazakhstan, Uzbekistan, and Georgia. In the late 1980s, when the Soviet BW program reached its apogee, roughly 60,000 scientists, technicians, and other personnel worked on the development, weaponization, and production of biological weapons. Many of these individuals are now unemployed or underemployed and facing severe economic deprivation. As a result, they might be tempted by high salaries or other inducements to sell their deadly expertise to wealthy terrorist organizations or proliferant states. Indeed, anecdotal evidence suggests that several former Soviet bioweapons scientists are living and working in Iran.

In an effort to reduce this threat, the United States and other governments are providing grants for peaceful research to former Soviet BW scientists through the International Science and Technology Center in Moscow and other "biological engagement" programs. To date, however, the level of funding allocated to this purpose has not been commensurate with the seriousness of the threat. In addition, South African BW specialists who worked for the apartheid-era Project Coast may also be susceptible to recruitment.

Reducing the Risks

The historical record suggests that there is an inverse relationship between the likelihood and scale of future bioterrorist attacks. Small-scale incidents such as the anthrax letters will probably occur again and cause limited damage, whereas worst-case events such as a smallpox epidemic are much less likely but potentially catastrophic. Public health specialists at Johns Hopkins University have argued that if even a single case of smallpox were diagnosed in the United States, the nation's entire air transport system would have to be shut down for as long as a month to prevent infected people from rapidly spreading the disease nationwide. The vast economic consequences of such a step suggest the possible multiplier effects of even a medium-scale bioterrorist attack.

How can we make it more difficult for terrorists to get their hands on dangerous disease agents? Since 1997, the CDC has monitored transfers of certain listed microbial pathogens and toxins from one U.S. laboratory to another. The problem is that the existing law has a major loophole: Labs are not required to register with the CDC if they merely hold or work with the listed pathogens but do not transfer them. Recently, Congress passed legislation to regulate possession as well as transfers of the listed pathogens, with the aim of ensuring that only legitimate scientists are given access to these dangerous materials.

A related problem is that the roughly 1,500 culture collections around the world that provide or sell microorganisms for scientific and pharmaceutical research are not well regulated. During the late 1980s, for example, Iraq obtained BW agents from the United States under false pretenses. Iraqi government scientists claiming to be engaged in legitimate public health research ordered seed cultures of anthrax bacteria and other pathogens from a leading U.S. biological supply company. The Department of Commerce approved the shipments, which found their way into the Iraqi BW program. This cautionary tale suggests the need for international restrictions on access to dangerous pathogens, as well as universal standards for the physical security and biosafety of microbial culture collections. Imposing such regulations uniformly around the world will require the negotiation of a "biosecurity convention" that is legally binding on all participating countries.

Because prevention of bioterrorism is desirable but not foolproof, it must be backed up with plans for consequence management in the event of a successful attack. Health care practitioners and emergency planners must be prepared for a wide range of contingencies. It is essential not to focus exclusively on worst-case scenarios but to prepare for the more likely small-scale incidents. The types of biological attack for which the technical hurdles are fairly low include the delivery of limited amounts of agent (as in the anthrax letter attacks), releases of aerosolized agent in an enclosed space (such as a subway station or a shopping mall), and contamination of food and beverages.

Many microbial pathogens are delivered most easily in food. In September 1984, for example, members of the Rajneeshee religious cult in Oregon poured salmonella (food-poisoning) bacteria on restaurant salad bars at ten restaurants in the small town of The Dalles. The motive for the attack was to test a scheme to manipulate the outcome of a local election in the cult's favor by making many of the town's residents temporarily too sick to vote. As it happened, more than 750 citizens of The Dalles contracted food poisoning, and an unknown number of out-of-towners who stopped to eat at one of the contaminated restaurants may also have been affected. Although state and Federal public health authorities investigated the salmonellosis outbreak, they concluded that it was natural in origin. Only a year later, when a cult member confessed to the crime, did the real cause become known.

For most bioterrorist incidents, the first line of defense will be at the local and state levels. Beyond stockpiling drugs and vaccines, it is crucial that physicians learn to diagnose exotic infectious diseases such as anthrax or smallpox at an early stage, when they are still readily treatable or containable with vaccination. For example, because the initial appearance of a smallpox rash closely resembles that of chickenpox, a relatively benign disease, health practitioners must be trained to recognize the subtle differences between them.

The U.S. public health infrastructure has been allowed to atrophy over the past few decades, making it essential to remedy serious deficiencies in city, county, and state health departments. Critical needs include improved staff coverage at night and on weekends, so that physicians can report unusual outbreaks of disease on a 24/7 basis. Improved communications systems and coordination mechanisms will also be required so that local, state, and Federal public health authorities can be linked together into a seamless web. To the extent possible, the strategies used to address bioterrorism should be suitable for responding to natural outbreaks of infectious disease. For example, improving epidemiological surveillance and response capabilities around the country would make the nation better prepared for the full range of infectious disease threats, of which bioterrorism is only one.

Conclusion

The tragic events of autumn 2001 have forced policy analysts to reassess their assessments of the likelihood of bioterrorism. Although the anthrax letter attacks were limited in scale, recent years have seen ominous developments along all three dimensions of the bioterrorism threat: motivation, organization, and technical capability. These developments suggest that the threat of bioterrorism is real and growing. U.S. health professionals must educate themselves about this emerging threat so they are prepared to respond effectively if and when our worst nightmares become a reality.

Chapter Three

The National Response: Options, Opportunities, Operations

Donald A. Henderson, MD, MPH

T his paper reviews the U.S. attitude toward preparing for bioterrorism—before and after September 11—and the accelerated efforts
now underway to counter the threat posed by bioterrorists. I write
it drawing from experience in the field of public health (for example, direct-
ing the World Health Organization campaign to eradicate smallpox); in the
Federal government service as an advisor on science and technology; and,
currently, as director of the Office of Public Health Preparedness at the
Department of Health and Human Services (HHS).

The Truth Unfolds

It was only in 1991, two years after Dr. Ken Alibek had left Russia where he
had been involved in making an antibiotic-resistant plague organism suitable for biological weapons, that the United States had the first real knowledge that the Russians had a biological weapons program. It came as a
tremendous surprise. As we were later to learn, that program had reached
the level of about 60,000 people working in some fifty different laboratories
and employing some of the very best people in biology. It had been in existence for a long time.

At the time this information was being unearthed, there was limited
expertise in either the public health or the medical arenas in the United
States about biological weapons and their potential, and there were not

many people with expertise in the diseases considered to pose the greatest risk. At Johns Hopkins University, the idea of even taking contracts from the Aberdeen Proving Grounds that related in any way to chemical weapons, even those involving nonclassified material, was poorly regarded by faculty; several contracts were turned down even though they were not classified contracts. It was certainly a holdover, in part, from Vietnam. There was also a feeling that the healing arts should not be concerned with these kinds of weapons.

In 1991, HHS wanted to brief the staff at the Centers for Disease Control and Prevention (CDC) on potential risks in the civilian sector, only to find no one with a top-secret security clearance at CDC. In the office of the HHS secretary, there was not even a secure fax to use.

Some Defining Moments

The question is, What has changed and when did it change? I believe that the nation started to pay attention to the possibility of a bioweapons attack after three watershed events in 1995.

First, in that year, terrorists released the gas saran in the Tokyo subway. As we were later to learn, they had also tried to aerosolize anthrax throughout the city on a number of different occasions, using a commercial vehicle and a commercial spray device. The one mistake they made was to use a vaccine strain of anthrax rather than a lethal strain. Consequently, there were not the hundreds of thousands of casualties that likely would have happened had they used a different strain of anthrax. The terrorists had also sent a team of more than twenty people to Zaire (now the Democratic Republic of the Congo) to obtain specimens for use from the Ebola outbreaks. (The United States had inspectors working throughout Iraq that same year.)

Second, Saddam Hussein's son-in-law defected, delivering what became known as the "chicken coop papers." This stack of material demonstrated that Iraq had a far more sophisticated, far more elaborate system for their biological weapons production than we had guessed.

At that point, one had to ask: If we know so little about Iraq despite all the inspection we were doing there, what might be going on in other countries, for example, North Korea, Iran, Syria, or Sudan? This conjecture elicited a good deal of alarm.

Third, the information from Ken Alibek became widely available within government. Defecting in December 1992, he had been the Number Two man in the entire biological weapons program of the Soviet Union. He brought with him an incredible tale of a huge operation, so incredible that he was not believed for a while. But, gradually, there was confirmation of much of what he reported.

In 1980, as Alibek described it, and coincident with the determination that smallpox had been eradicated and vaccination could cease, the USSR began an intensive program to produce the smallpox virus. It is quite clear from his descriptions of their difficulties and how they solved them that it was a legitimate effort. The Soviets eventually got to the point of having a smallpox production facility, which could turn out between 80 and 100 tons of smallpox in a year. Along with plague and anthrax, it was intended for use on an intercontinental ballistic missile (for strategic purposes, as they described it), with multiple reentry warheads that would get down near the ground, break apart, and disseminate an aerosol over a wide area.

The secret plant where they made the smallpox is about forty or fifty miles outside Moscow. It is still in existence. It is totally out of bounds; no one is permitted to enter. There are three other plants, all under the Ministry of Defense, where a number of activities are clearly being hidden. What is going on, we really do not know.

The First U.S. Response to Potential Threats

These three events led to President Clinton issuing a Presidential Decision Directive in 1995, a classified document that went to each of the cabinet departments. In it, he discussed the need for the departments to begin preparing and planning to deal with issues of terrorism, particularly biological terrorism. The Defense Against Weapons of Mass Destruction Act (the Nunn-Lugar-Domenici amendment to the National Defense Authorization Act) was passed in 1996, calling for training teams in 120 cities; this training went ahead and is still somewhat in place. It is intended to train first-responders: police, fire, and emergency rescue people. The primary focus was on dealing with an explosive or chemical incident. In fact, the term used very commonly was *chembio*. The assumption was that if you know how to deal with a chemical incident, you automatically know how to deal with a biologic incident.

When a chemical or explosive incident occurs, you know it immediately. You need the flashing lights and the sirens to stabilize the situation, and start evacuation, decontamination, and other relevant tasks. However, these events are nothing like a biologic incident in which an aerosol is released, and you do not know that anything has happened for days or weeks. In such a case, first-responders are the people in the emergency rooms, the public health arena, and the laboratories. They were not included in any of the early training activities. The HHS asked for nothing, and they got nothing: Its FY 1997 budget was miniscule compared to the billions of dollars going to the Departments of Defense, Energy, and Justice.

In 1997, Michael Osterholm, director of the Center for Infectious Disease Research and Policy, the University of Minnesota; Richard Preston, who wrote *The Cobra Event*, a fictionalized story of a biological weapon attack, and *The Hot Zone*, an account of the Ebola virus; and I decided that we needed to educate the medical and public health communities about terrorism threats and get to the Congress and the Executive Branch to say, "We have a problem." We started at the Infectious Diseases Society meeting in San Francisco in Fall 1997, followed by a series of invitations to speak at grand rounds in many places and to different professional groups. Gradually, some appreciation of the problem took hold, along with a sense that a greatly strengthened infrastructure was needed to cope with a potential crisis. We needed a stronger public health component with appropriate links, particularly to emergency rooms and hospitals. We needed a network of laboratories to diagnose bioweapons because laboratories are not normally prepared to do this. Fundamentally, we needed a structure to deal with any major catastrophic event calling for a surge capacity. If, for example, the United States had had the H5N1 flu as was the case in Hong Kong, with its eighteen cases and six deaths, and it had spread out of its confines, where would the United States have been given the trouble we have dealing with a mild influenza outbreak? In May 1998 the President proposed that the HHS budget be increased substantially. However, hospitals and academic health centers were still little involved.

The Center for Civilian Biodefense Strategies

At the Center for Civilian Biodefense Strategies at Johns Hopkins University, which I helped found, the hope was to use the center as a possible means of communication. We then sought some help from foundations that normally fund public health and medical initiatives, but were told by all that biodefense was a difficult subject and they did not think their trustees would want to fund something in this area. The arms control people said they had never funded anything in a school of medicine or public health. "We really do not know what you are like."

Thus, for almost two years, the center basically existed on fumes. It was difficult getting a message across with only a part-time staff, but we did as best we could, also utilizing donated time and effort. In June 2001, the staff wrote a scenario, "Dark Winter," for a smallpox epidemic. With two other organizations, the center put on a table-top exercise at Andrews Air Force Base, with important policy makers participating. Former Senator Sam Nunn (D-Ga.) took the role of President. John Hamery, under secretary of defense, played the part of the secretary of defense. Margaret Hamburg, former assistant secretary of health, took the role of the secretary of health. Jim Miklescweski represented the television side, and Judith Miller represented the *New York Times*. Both Nunn and Hamery each reported separately that they had no idea of the extent of the problem that an outbreak of disease could pose.

Sam Nunn also informed the audience that he was setting up the Nuclear Threat Initiative funded by Ted Turner. (It immediately became a program for both nuclear and biologic threats.) He then asked the Congress to hold hearings on the possibility of such attacks, at which Hamery and he subsequently testified. The last hearing was with the Senate Foreign Relations Committee on September 5, and it drew the attention of Congress as never before.

Anthrax Comes to the Post Office

September 11 came and, shortly thereafter, there was a rumor of a second possible event. At the center, we came to the conclusion that it was unlikely to involve an airplane; the agent would be anthrax. This conclusion was reached because various newspaper articles in Middle East papers and statements made by those who might be involved, including Al Qaeda, were talking about using anthrax against American bases and people in the Middle East.

The Office of Public Health Preparedness

On the second of October came the first case of anthrax. On the first of November, the Office of Public Health Preparedness was created at HHS. The secretary wanted one program, instead of the approximately seven or eight different programs at CDC, most of which did not talk to each other. The Health Resources and Services Administration (HRSA) also had a totally separate operation, as did the National Institutes of Health (NIH) and the Food and Drug Administration (FDA), who were each beginning to put money into the research side. None of this was coordinated. The plan was for the Office of Public Health Preparedness to not only coordinate these various activities, but also to direct the program. No funds were to be released for any of the programs until they were reviewed and judged to meet requirements.

The Office of Public Health Preparedness is guided by three watch words: *speed* in making the funds immediately available, *flexibility* in how the funds are to be used, and *accountability* where there are guidelines for use of the funds.

We had been assured that getting money out to the states would require at least four to six months. The Office of Health Preparedness did it in three weeks, putting out more than $1 billion to the states. The office then began an intensive program with a series of priorities, trying to move as quickly as possible so that the United States could be in a position to respond to an attack. Meanwhile, the office continued to work with the anthrax episode hanging over our heads.

The recognition today is that all terrorism is local and, for an effective national response, there must be an effective local and state response. There is a tendency at the Department of Defense to believe sufficient defense assets or assets mobilized from outside the local area would have a major impact. But localities have many people who know their own area very well, along with a local structure and organization. Federal assets can be brought in to help in various ways, but they have to fit into a local structure.

At present, the Office of Public Preparedness has broad oversight of national and some state and local activities. For about three years, a limited amount of money had been going to the states, but it was no more than $45–50 million altogether. Spread across the states and local communities, it did not amount to much. However, it did provide the impetus for many of them to take some steps toward preparedness. The Office of Public Preparedness brought together about ten of the funding streams going to the states. The idea was to give the states flexibility and the office an opportunity to move much more quickly than before.

In 1980, vaccinating against smallpox stopped throughout the world. It had been halted in the United States in 1972. At least 45 percent of the U.S. population is not vaccinated, and it is estimated that those vaccinated only once before 1972 probably have little immunity now. This makes 80 percent of the U.S. population fully susceptible.

Meanwhile, vaccine production has stopped worldwide. It had been produced by scarifying the flank of a calf, letting it grow for six or seven days, then sanguinating it, scraping off the material that was there, and straining it to get the hair out of it. It was then bottled. It was somewhat crude as a product, but it did a good job of stopping the spread of the disease.

We have now moved to making vaccine out of tissue cell culture and it has been a very active program. We will have 250 million doses by December 2002. Meanwhile, 15 million doses are available, or roughly the equivalent of 140,000 to 150,000 vials. Studies show that it could be diluted five-fold. We could probably vaccinate 50 million people if we were really put to it as an interim measure.

The anthrax vaccine is made, at present, by a fairly old method in which the whole organism is broken up. The U.S. Army Medical Research Detachment (USAMRD) is developing a recombinant vaccine, which has been put on fast track; we have hopes that it will be available within eighteen months. This would permit a two- to three-dose schedule for immunization. It should be virtually without side effects.

We have obtained sufficient anthrax antibiotics to treat roughly twenty million people for sixty days. With surge capacities in the various pharmaceutical companies, we feel reasonably well covered. The antibiotics are in twelve push-packages in different parts of the country. We can get a package to a site anywhere in the country in twelve hours. They were used in the New York episode, with a package arriving in about six hours. Whatever the situation, the push-packages can be delivered. By having them under good control, with good stewardship, it will be a good product when it goes out, and should replace many different packages in different states controlled many times in inadequate ways. In addition, the current network of about 80 laboratories will probably expand to about 100 laboratories. They will have the same protocols and re-agents, and be in a position to be tested regularly through the year so that a rapid diagnosis for exotic agents can be made in a number of places.

Need for Surge Capacity

There is now a key need to involve both the academic health sector and the hospitals in emergency health preparedness. The HHS appropriation of $125 million, spread over five thousand hospitals, amounts to $20,000 to $25,000 per hospital, not very much money, and poses a real challenge, especially in these times.

The need for surge capacity for patients in the event of a major outbreak requires regional planning. Hospitals do not get together very often to deal with common issues; there is some element of competition among them. Neither have hospitals and health departments customarily worked together. Nevertheless, the Office of Health Preparedness is asking health systems throughout the country to look at regional planning for dealing with surge capacity for patients. For example, perhaps the accommodations for some patients in Veterans Administration (VA) hospitals who are not very sick could be compressed a bit. The VA also has some buildings not being used. We would like to see military, VA, and other hospitals get together to decide how to best deal initially with a surge of perhaps 500 patients over a short period of time. Meanwhile, the Center for Public Health Preparedness will be surveying what hospitals really need in the event of a biological, chemical, or radiological situation. Given the amount of money available, preparation could at least be made to assure that febrile patients coming into emergency rooms can be isolated or separated from other patients until some sort of determination is made about what brought them there.

The President's budget for FY 2003 has about $550 million for hospitals. Senator Bill Frist (R-Tenn.) does not think the hospitals should have more money. I think that, given the hospitals' commitment to provide both a social good and medical care, there has to be some provision and some payment system to assure that the hospitals are prepared to deal with a major outbreak from whatever source.

Meanwhile, it would be useful for hospitals to have enough antibiotics to cover their staff and families for forty-eight hours. They do not need a huge stock. Probably they could use a stock that is manageable with a rotating inventory rather than try to get a large amount of antibiotics and then lose out on antibiotics put away, not used, and expiring.

Conclusion

The strength of the local structure is going to depend on how well the nation responds to a bioterrorist attack. Thus, emphasis on the state and local areas is of critical importance. The timeliness and the quality of the initial engagement will determine a great deal about the severity of the crisis. Early detection, early diagnosis, and early response are key and can make a big difference.

Academic health centers in many parts of the country are in a position to provide real leadership in this regard, both in educating heath professionals and the public and in organizing the response effort. The emphasis should be on the larger hospitals, which have the larger labor pools and probably more flexibility than small rural and local hospitals. Much has to be developed locally, and each geographic area will be different, depending on the different arrangements the hospitals and the local health departments make with each other and the strategies they devise for enlisting volunteers. But, where else would one find people better equipped for the job than at the academic health centers?

Chapter Four

The HHS Agenda: Priorities and Choices

Eve Slater, MD

C learly during the last several months, the heroes of the events at the World Trade Center and the Pentagon, and in Somerset County, Pennsylvania, have been health care professionals, from the first responders to the veterinarians and morticians who dedicated their time to helping the nation recover. Both the U.S. Department of Health and Human Services (HHS) and the Bush Administration are now committed to providing the highest level of medical resources to the American people and are moving on a number of fronts.

The health care community is also continuing to help prepare America in the event of additional attacks. Readiness is essential, and the partnership between academic health centers and the Federal government is irreplaceable. This paper outlines some of the agendas of the HHS secretary and the President, and some of the critical decisions about emergency preparedness that are most likely to rest in the hands of academic health center leaders.

Shoring Up Health Resources

Should another terrorist attack occur, one with a biological vector, the many affected individuals will probably be brought to academic health centers. These institutions, as centers of tertiary care, may in fact become rapidly involved. It is also likely that as bioterrorism and public health infrastructure monies become available, some of the decisions regarding the triage of those monies will fall to academic health centers. Thus, these major health institutions must focus attention as directly as possible on shoring up infrastructure by region and territory and by preparing locally for an event. It is equally important for academic health centers sharing in the decisions on the allocation of monies to keep in mind the overall public health infrastructure because every health institution is dealing with similar dilemmas.

Integrating HHS and Private Sector Planning

Since Secretary Thompson arrived in Washington, he has assembled an elite group of doctors, scientists, and bioterrorism experts. Dr. Donald Henderson is spearheading the efforts at the Office of Public Health Preparedness to implement the money granted by the President and Congress to prevent and respond to bioterrorism. The Food and Drug Administration (FDA), the Centers for Disease Control and Prevention (CDC), and the National Institutes of Health (NIH) are also dedicated to the bioterrorism effort. The President has been keenly focused on preventing bioterrorism, and he has given the responsibility for coordinating the activities of all governmental health-related agencies to my office, the Office of the Assistant Secretary at HHS.

Initially, $1.5 billion was released to strengthen prevention of and responsiveness to bioterrorism as part of the $40 billion Homeland Defense Package approved by Congress. The NIH has thus begun research on a new, improved anthrax vaccine and on vaccines for plague and hemorrhagic fevers. The HHS has purchased sufficient doses of smallpox vaccine, some of which are available now, some of which will be available within the next calendar year. There will be enough for every man, woman, and child in the United States.

Four vaccine manufacturers in the United States have a near-monopoly on producing many of the vaccines needed for disease prevention. The government, generally speaking, does not like to take on production responsibilities. On the other hand, the government may become interested in taking on some of the production of vaccines for very rare diseases if the private sector cannot be induced to do so.

If one manufacturer encounters a difficulty because vaccines are difficult to produce, the United States experiences shortages. The National Childhood Vaccine Injury Compensation Act of 1986 revitalized vaccine production, and there are now several legislative attempts to revitalize that bill.

HHS is working to strengthen all facets of the public health system. This effort includes improved training for emergency room physicians, nurses, and other health care professionals who may be called upon to deal with chemical and biological attacks. For the FDA, the President has requested $61 million to enhance the frequency and quality of imported food inspections and modernize the import data system for detecting tainted food. This funding will also provide 410 new FDA inspectors to help ensure that the food supply is better protected, particularly at U.S. borders.

Health Alert Network

At the state level, governments are receiving almost $1 billion to help them strengthen their capacity to respond to bioterrorism and other public health emergencies that might be related to terrorism. The HHS is working with CDC on the Health Alert Network, a project to connect state and major county health systems electronically. It is about twenty feet away from the secretary's office and operates twenty-four hours a day, seven days a week, and was operative during the height of the anthrax attacks and during the Olympics. The command center receives all information on potential bioterrorist attacks and decides how to act on the information.

The anthrax attack has troubled everyone, and five people died. Yet many thousands of individuals received medications and were offered vaccinations to keep them safe from exposure to the disease. An article in *Science* magazine estimated that the distribution of antibiotics likely prevented anywhere from two to five times the number of cases of anthrax seen.

In the wake of the anthrax attacks, the hoaxes and the mistaken reports were a tremendous drain on local responders, the academic health centers, and the Federal government agencies trying to track down a number of these reports. On September 11, the command center was responsible for rushing a push-pack containing fifty tons of medicines, vaccines, and equipment to New York; it arrived within seven hours of the first tower catastrophe. Public health personnel, ranging from triage physicians to mortuary experts and veterinarians, worked around the clock in New York City and at the Pentagon. All these actions were taken efficiently, quickly, and effectively.

Coordination with Homeland Security Office

The Homeland Security Office has delegated most health issues directly to Secretary Thompson, whose department works with Federal agencies to coordinate efforts and avoid duplication of work. For example, HHS and the

Department of Defense (DoD) are working on projects to promote the development of vaccines to treat rare diseases, vaccines that both departments hope remain on the shelves to be used primarily as deterrents. The HHS is also working with DoD, NIH, the operating divisions within the Federal government, and the private sector to formulate arrangements for stockpiling vaccines and other pharmaceuticals.

Reserve Corps of Health Care Professionals

The HHS is well aware of the scarcity of reserves to deal with a significant health emergency and the need to encourage health care professionals to volunteer to serve during such emergencies. The President is arguing for supporting the establishment of a medical reserve corps within the new USA Freedom Corps, which is designed to promote volunteerism. The framework for the medical reserve unit will be the revitalized Commissioned Corps of the Public Health Service. There are approximately 6,000 active people in the corps, but many have been deployed to areas that are not necessarily the first line of response for acts of terrorism. Many are assigned to American Indian reservations and prisons, where it has been difficult to recruit medical professionals.

The HHS is also planning to improve training facilities. The emphasis will be on training health care professionals to deal with bioterrorism. The training will be available to the members of the corps and to the uniformed services. Many courses will be held in conjunction with the schools of public health and academic health centers to train people who are not, per se, members of the corps but will be involved in emergency response.

Budget Initiatives

Bioterrorism

In general terms, the FY 2002 budget for public health is generous. However, the monies must be spent wisely and appropriately. The philosophy has always been to leave the primary responsibility for the monies to the states. The Governors are being given the primary responsibility for allocating Federal funds because the first response to any act of terrorism will happen at the regional and local interface.

Biomedical Research

HHS is also advancing important biomedical research. The budget provides $5.5 billion for cancer research and $2.8 billion for HIV/AIDS research. Another $1 billion, funded from several sources within and outside NIH, is allocated to addressing the global health issues of AIDS, tuberculosis, and malaria.

Welfare and Medicaid

The Administration's activities to prepare low-income Americans for their future are expansive. Seven million fewer persons are on welfare today, and 2.8 million fewer children live in poverty, in large part because welfare has been transformed. The President's budget requires HHS to work closely with the states to help low-income Americans who have left welfare climb the career ladder. The foundation of successful welfare reform is work, the only way to leave poverty and become in dependent. The President's budget allocates $16.5 billion for block grant funding. This funding provides supplemental grants to address historical disparities in welfare spending among states and strengthens work-participation requirements. States have the flexibility to mix effective education and job training programs with work and the money to strengthen families and reduce illegitimacy. Additionally, the budget provides $350 million additional dollars for Medicaid benefits for those low-income Americans in transition from welfare to work. The President is calling for a continued commitment to childcare that includes $2.7 billion for entitlement childcare funding and $2.1 billion for discretionary funding.

Medicare

Strengthening Medicare is another key component of the effort to broaden and strengthen the country's health care system. The FY 2003 budget dedicates $190 billion over ten years for targeted improvements in comprehensive Medicare modernization. The modernization includes a subsidized prescription-drug benefit, better insurance protection, and better private options for all beneficiaries.

The Uninsured

As the government reaches out to people still relying on welfare and works to strengthen Medicare, we cannot ignore the roughly 40 million Americans who are reported to lack health insurance. Since January 2001, the government has approved state plan amendments, Medicaid, and State Child Health Insurance Program (SCHIP) waivers that have expanded the opportunity for health coverage to 1.8 million Americans and improved existing benefits to 4.5 million individuals. The President's budget also includes $89 billion in new health credits to help American families buy health insurance. These credits will provide health coverage for many low-income families.

Patient Safety

Secretary Thompson is also committed to improving patient safety. The total HHS budget for this effort is $84 million in 2003. The Institute of Medicine recently documented that as many as 98,000 Americans die annually due to medical errors. In the 2003 budget, President Bush has proposed $10 million in new funding to improve patient safety and reduce medical errors, primarily through informatics systems. The office of the assistant secretary is also involved with initiatives for proper education in the use of medications. The funds for patient safety will also help promote wider use of safety technologies, and develop new approaches to, and support a stronger system for, rapid reporting of adverse medical events.

Conclusion

Thus, HHS is moving forward across the board, working with the non-govermental health sector, including academic health centers, to help guarantee that America is ready for every contingency. Emergency preparedness will go a long way toward negating and eliminating risk and harm. Although the future is uncertain, it is useful to read the words of Samuel Adams, a signer of the Declaration of Independence:

> The freedom of our civil constitution is worth defending at all hazards, and it is our duty to defend it against all attacks.

The HHS feels that it is winning in this regard.

Chapter Five

Pharmaceuticals: Supplies, Stockpiles, and Systems in Crisis

Henri R. Manasse Jr., PhD, ScD

T his paper discusses the issues and implications of pharmaceutical supply and demand in the event of a national emergency. It is purposely pragmatic, grounded in what is going on and what is possible. The focus is on the multidisciplinary aspects of the situation because the medication supply process—starting with the manufacturer, proceeding to the prescriber, to the distributor, and to the patient—involves many parties.

Federal Planning

The Department of Health and Human Services (HHS) has an all-hazards approach to the nation's pharmaceutical supply that takes into account the various chemical agents, vaccines, and other biologics that might be needed in the event of mass casualties. Emergency scenarios could involve chemical- and biological-agent fission and contaminated nuclear materials, explosives, and natural disasters. The pharmaceutical agents do not involve only anti-infective agents but also a number of drugs and vaccines that would be routinely used to maintain and manage emergency situations. They include a number of other significant drugs in short supply: anesthetic agents, neuromuscular blocking agents, and other agents that, in case of emergencies, the academic health centers absolutely must have.

For mass-casualty treatment and prevention, a series of pharmaceutical agents typically are used. In the case of radiation, it is potassium iodide;

nerve agents require nerve and chemical agent antidotes. Epidemics thus call for a variety of very specific vaccines.

Academic health centers, therefore, should question fundamental planning assumptions at their facilities. First, what supply levels of routine pharmaceutical agents and supplies are normally on hand? Then, what quantities and emergency products are needed to ensure adequate surge capacity? (Staff in the emergency room, pharmacy department, and surgical suites are unable to give a clear answer to either query.) The third question is whether the institution needs stockpiles or information on other solutions to keeping supply levels stable.

The Drug-Supply Chain

The United States has significant assets: about 180,000 practicing pharmacists and 60,000 pharmacies in hospitals, community-based operations, and a variety of other sites serving close to 180 million people. However, the complexity of the pharmaceutical process hinders responses to an interruption in production or supply, and affects issues like shortages. In addition, the pharmacy field in the United States does not have a volunteer enlistment system, although one is being discussed as part of overall citywide and statewide planning activities.

The basic, or short, version of the pharmaceutical chain involves (1) the manufacturer (supplier), (2) a distribution system, and (3) the end user. (The long version appears in figure 1.) If the United States excels at and is superior in anything, it is this dramatic and incredible system that can supply pharmaceutical agents in a just-in-time phenomenon across this country to 280 million people. This system has carried necessary pharmaceutical agents, without disruption, to disasters such as Hurricane Andrew in Florida and the Oklahoma bombing incident.

A few years ago, the White House brought together the entire pharmacy community—e.g., manufacturers, distributors, and hospital pharmacy directors—to begin to plan for the year 2000. At the time, there was immense concern as to whether the supply system would break down if all the computers broke down, and for about a year and a half, the pharmaceutical community and policymakers had rather intensive discussions. Although nothing happened to the computers, everyone was well assured that the supply system would retain its integrity, notwithstanding the possibility that computers might not be working.

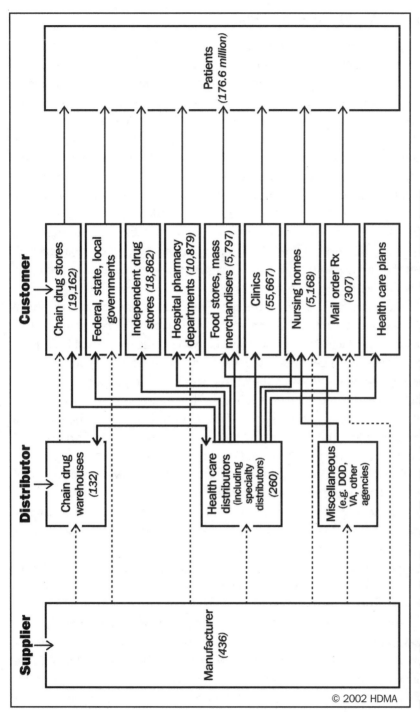

Figure 1. Pharmaceutical Product Flow Map (over a 90-day inventory period), 2001–2002

© 2002 HDMA

Supply System Vulnerabilities

However, there are some vulnerabilities in the system as it stands today. First, the country has no overarching national plan. Obviously, in a capitalistic society, pharmaceutical agents are treated like any other commodity in the marketplace. Although there is a very broad definition of medical necessity in Food and Drug Administration (FDA) law, the law does not give the FDA much authority to force manufacturers to manufacture anything. Fundamentally, there are no overarching production or stockpiling quotas and, thus, no overall knowledge of where any of the products are, how they are managed, or how they are controlled. The American Society of Health-System Pharmacists (ASHP) and the industry leadership have looked at the various disasters and concluded: "We responded in an unorganized, organized way." However, if there had been simultaneous, multisite attacks all over the country with a number of casualties, one would question whether or not things would have been all right.

Manufacturing is an extremely complex scientific and technical process, and it can take up to a year to manufacture a drug from scratch. Vaccine manufacturing is especially costly. Also, there are significant business issues and incentives that must be addressed by everyone. Some of the vulnerabilities associated with the supply chain include communication gaps and parochial barriers. Local entities such as public health agencies, emergency management officials, first-responders, health care institutions and schools, and health professionals and other professional scientists may all be involved and even create barriers.

Public health agencies, for example, do not have a very good sense of supply-chain vulnerabilities, partly because ensuring the integrity of this chain is not a first priority for them, and many do not have a pharmacy expert on staff. Community emergency-management officials usually look at pharmaceutical supplies as a last resort. Neither is there much cross-discussion in health sciences centers, which is particularly disturbing for an issue that requires across-the-channel dialogue. Also important are discussions among professional societies.

Another vulnerability lies in this country's dependence on production elsewhere. About 80 percent of the raw materials from which pharmaceutical agents are manufactured come from outside the United States. Some countries have political vulnerabilities, making the supply chain vulnerable with regard to raw materials. The United States also manufactures finished goods in other countries; these have to be moved into the United States. Thus, even the issue of how quickly the U.S. Customs Department gets into gear to move these products out of warehouses and release them back into the supply chain needs examination.

Inventory Systems

As a consequence of many of the cost pressures that hospitals face these days, institutions have gone to just-in-time inventory, that is, the day you want a product is the day you get it. This system means that manufacturers only produce for just-in-time inventories in wholesale distribution warehouses. The distributors are only housing for just-in-time deliveries. Ultimately, hospitals have on hand only what they can use for that day. Aided by automation, it has evolved into common practice, reducing space and budget requirements on the part of the provider. However, because the inventory is static, the situation creates a significant problem when hospitals need surge capacity of rather dramatic inventories.

It is not atypical for a hospital pharmacy to carry about 3,000 drug products. (Translate this number into what the pharmaceuticals cost, and a $50 million inventory is not unlikely.) The system is similar to a beltway with cars going sixty-five miles an hour with only about one foot between each car. If a driver suddenly jams on the brakes, there is a significant, immediate impact on the traffic flow. Similarly, any disruption in flow of pharmaceuticals (whether from the production or distribution end) in an emergency medical situation will swiftly have an impact on patient care.

The scene in other countries should provide a dramatic wake-up call. In Uzbekistan, insulin is not available. Emergency rooms do not have anesthetic or paralytic agents normally used in emergency rooms. The entire supply-chain infrastructure was torn apart with the dissolution of the Soviet Union. Czechoslovakia, East Germany, and Hungary were the primary producers of pharmaceutical agents for the entire USSR; when it fell apart, they said, "We don't want your rubles anymore."

Drug shortages have become a significant public health issue. It is not just an issue of logistics, production, manufacturing, or distribution; there are a variety of causes. The problem appeared about two years ago when Wyeth decided to stop producing tetanus. Some people were tempted to direct anger at the manufacturer. There were questions: Has the FDA shut Wyeth down? Has the company decided there is not enough profit in tetanus? There is no simple answer to these questions. There is no simple answer to any of the shortage issues.

What are some of the shortages? First are the raw materials; these must be tested, evaluated, and embargoed, a complex process associated with moving raw materials into the manufacturing process. Sometimes manufacturing difficulties are involved in shortages. The FDA has stepped up enforcement in a number of manufacturing areas, and companies that historically may not have had regulatory problems have begun to see complications. It may mean that a company shuts the line down and stops manufacturing.

The business climate has had an effect. An immense number of mergers have occurred in the pharmaceutical industry, even as new generic companies have come on board. However, unless a certain amount of profit can be guaranteed, it is difficult to maintain a complex manufacturing enterprise. One of the concerns about the expansion is whether sufficient technical and scientific talent is available to staff pharmaceutical laboratories and production centers. The country has seen decreased inventories and safety stocks because of corporate financial pressures; the decreasing number of organizations in the industry; and the continuously growing problems with vaccines and antibiotic production, the complex products in our supply chain.

Organizations are looking at therapeutic alternatives in case drugs are in short supply or not available. As a result, some organizations are sharing this information widely with purchasing agents and others involved in distribution. More information on drug shortages appears on the ASHP Web site <<www.ashp.org/shortage>>. Tracking shortages has almost become a full-time job for a staff member at ASHP. The country is currently short about forty drugs (some are vaccines), and the list grows every day. The Web site indicates if there is resolution.

Stockpiling

When it comes to stockpiling, two important terms come into play: "static stockpile" and "dynamic inventory." There are some significant shortcomings to a static stockpile, which basically is drugs sitting in a warehouse somewhere, whether in a carrier truck or a container that goes onto a Boeing-747, significantly draining the supply chain.

There are twelve push-packs now, worth about $50 million each. We do not know what is in them because they are covered under security rules. Nevertheless, lots of drugs are sitting in these major push-packs, to say nothing of what is sitting in warehouses, the military, Veterans Administration (VA), and local and state health facilities.

These drugs have special storage requirements: some need refrigeration, some freezing, and some absolutely no light. These are agents that require stability management, which is a function of temperature. The storage of pharmaceutical agents is complicated and cost inefficient; it would not be difficult to tie up tens of millions of dollars in inventories if we were to stockpile all over the country, in every hospital, in every academic health center, in every pharmacy, and in every home. Indeed, one concern with the Year 2000 transition was that people would begin to hoard drugs, and the country would exceed the capacity to manufacture. Compounding the problem is that, in many respects, pharmaceuticals are unstable products. They require dating. Dating, of course, requires replenishment.

One alternative to consider is "dynamic inventory planning," which starts with a constant supply-level across a community. It is not difficult for each academic health science center to be in communication with the pharmacy departments in all the hospitals and pharmacies in the community. Indeed, there is a way to get one's arms around what supplies everybody has, what everybody has access to, and how quickly these products can be delivered so that they can be regularly replenished by manufacturers.

There is integrity in the supply-management system that allows one to get products into this dynamic inventory. FedEx, for example, has special dispensation from the Federal Aviation Administration (FAA) to fly during times of national emergency. The company was allowed to fly to New York and Washington in the aftermath of 9/11 and the anthrax scare, and move goods into the supply line.

It is also important to constantly manage and monitor inventory because, unless one has special FDA dispensation, the law states that goods that expire may not be used. Although there is a fair amount of fungibility with expiration dates, from a scientific point of view, people have to pay attention to the integrity associated with these products. What does dynamic inventory planning require? First, it should be maintained and mobilized through advance planning and coordination among hospital pharmacists, regional distributors, local planning officials, metropolitan medical response systems, Federal authorities, the military, and the VA. This web of relationships needs to be developed throughout each community so they can have a dynamic inventory and properly manage it. This, in turn, means that academic centers will have to move out of their normal sphere of relationships to be more involved these issues.

Second, maintaining the dynamism of that inventory implies looking at what happens in the first twenty-four hours of any emergency. The appropriate entities have to be able to draw from local supplies so that various points of service—emergency departments, local storage facilities, regional distributors, and the state (which may bring in the Federal government) are stocked. Theoretically, planners must be able to manage that inventory for at least twenty-four hours. Then, they can put other measures in place.

Collaborating on a National Level

The Centers for Disease Control and Prevention (CDC), in collaboration with the Federal Emergency Management Agency (FEMA) and the Office of Emergency Preparedness (OEP), have developed a national pharmaceutical stockpile, that includes the push-packs and the vendor-managed inventory discussed immediately below. The details have not been released for security purposes, and it is difficult to plan the inventory if you do not know what inventory might be arriving. Nonetheless, the national pharmaceutical stockpile is available to states on request of the governor in the case of emergency.

There is also a relationship between the OEP and what is known as the "vendor-managed inventory." This inventory comprises threat-specific drug entities that manufacturers and vendors, joining together, can move out of their sectors, and that are in addition to the supplies, push-packs, and what is in storage at VA and other health facilities.

Role of the Pharmacy Department

It is important to understand that, based on some anticipation of unexpected needs, distributors do allocate a certain amount of inventory for emergencies. For example, in the 9/11 situation, a fair amount of supply moved into the New York City area based on best guesses as to what was going to be needed before Federal supplies arrived. Some of the experiences in both New York City and Washington, D.C., as well as the disasters in Florida and Oklahoma City, have been lessons well learned in terms of movement of supply.

Pharmacy departments can serve as a valuable resource to the academic health center contemplating emergency preparation. Certainly, developing a database to monitor some of the core supplies needed for emergencies is an obvious step. Deciding on some of the outlier supplies is a tougher local challenge, and will take place at the local level.

The ASHP is currently developing an e-mail network, and it hopes to soon have every hospital's pharmacy director on an e-mail link so that any additional information from the manufacturing, distribution, and supply communities and emergency preparedness people can be channeled immediately to the pharmacy departments. Academic health center pharmacy groups can serve as experts on some of the drug supply issues and also deal with the issue of drug shortages.

The Pharmaceutical Industry as a Leader

Pharmacy people should be seen as leaders; they bring to the table an expertise that is urgently required. Packaging, labeling, storage, and supply management are not only what they learn in school, but what they are involved in every day as a significant portion of their work. They also have access to drug information. One of the most frustrating features of the anthrax situation in Washington was the immediate identification, apparently by government officials, of Cipro as the agent of choice. Another problem was watching patients being handed small plastic bags containing Cipro without any information. Cipro is not exactly an innocuous drug, and not necessarily one to take for sixty days. Consideration of whether a patient was pregnant or had a problem in renal function was just not part of the distribution of this very powerful drug.

The ASHP has been engaged in two executive sessions behind closed doors with representatives from the manufacturing industry, the supply-chain industry, and the Federal government to identify the gaps and make commitments to each other to find out how to resolve the problem. They have made an immense amount of progress. They have agreed to make the results of these executive sessions available at <<www.ashp.org>>.

ASHP also has committed to creating an emergency-preparedness, online resource center. Pharmacists are involved in community-preparedness planning. Thus, a number of pharmacy organizations are pushing the medical community to become more engaged in local health departments, statewide health departments, and community-based planning because the pharmaceutical supply is such an integral part of the care and treatment of patients.

Discussions are also taking place among national associations about the kinds of concerted efforts medical societies might engage in to deal with a shortage of drugs. One of the current dialogues concerns whether or not the health system can build a real-time inventory management system that would allow health professionals to quickly ascertain which drugs are where and how many there are. In fact, there is some speculation that the U.S. government might not have had to go into negotiations with Bayer for 190 million doses of Cipro (ciprofloxacin hydrochloride) if it had taken a snapshot of all the Cipro available in the country across all sectors during the anthrax scare.

The Academic Health Center as a Leader

Academic health centers provide community leadership regarding drug information. The ASHP received thousands of calls from people in the Washington area about Cipro. Academic health centers and their resources should be available to explain pharmaceutical agents, including some of the risks associated with them and their proper use.

Risk-communication is a significant issue that demands an immense amount of sensitivity. How do academic health centers communicate the risk associated with a particular disaster problem or the treatment alternatives? As I watched what was going on at the Brentwood Post Office in Washington during the anthrax scare, I realized there was not sufficient communication about the risks associated with Cipro. It is not reasonable to assume people will use these therapies if they cannot understand the risks and benefits of using it.

Also important are research and public health data. The health community needs to build the evidence necessary to support a unified national response to a particular hazard. All the activities around the country should be brought together. The health community should begin to examine best practices, share those best practices, and perhaps begin to eliminate some of the myths.

The paucity of information on public health in the teaching of pharmacists may present an opportunity for academic health centers to look at this situation as an area for study. Procurement logistics, an extremely complicated issue in other industries as well as in the pharmaceutical industry, is an expertise that can be effectively taught at academic health centers. Academic health centers, for example, should understand losses to inventory. Consider how emergency medical technicians (EMTs) restore supplies in ambulances, usually through favors by emergency room departments. Certainly, public and private health institutions have a significant vulnerability in this area, as do the schools of health professions.

Academic health centers should create linkages with public health officials and get involved in the use of Federal funding. It is now possible to access some of the money that goes to the states specifically to look at pharmaceutical distribution issues. Metropolitan medical response systems now require that the pharmaceutical supply chain be addressed and that the appropriate expertise be part of grant-planning activities associated with such funding.

Another significant issue is staffing. Can the appropriate staff and medical students in the various health professions deal with supply issues in the wake of significant staff shortages? Pharmacies and hospitals already are running at about an 18 percent vacancy rate.

Academic health science centers can serve as an ethical nexus for a public debate on unanswerable questions. For example, is it possible to prepare for every possibility? Most health practitioners probably have a view on that, but the leadership of health science centers can facilitate engagement of communities on this particular point.

Conclusion

Making pharmaceuticals available to people across the United States is not an autonomous, independent activity; rather, it is one with an immense amount of interconnectivity. This aspect of the industry should be reinforced, particularly in light of the plans being considered at the Federal, state, and local levels for coping with major disasters.

What is the bottom line? What does the community need to do with regard to having enough pharmaceuticals in the event of a crisis? Having the basics on hand for the first twenty-four hours is key. After that, the local health community should rely on relationships set up with other health resources, including the VA, military bases, the CDC, and OEP. Pharmacy expertise and communitywide planning for medication supply needs should be integrated. Thinking and planning for a dynamic inventory, rather than stockpiling per se, is important.

How much can the country afford to spend? Take the $600 million worth of push-packs sitting in steel containers. Add that to the list of other expenditures associated with emergency preparedness. The total investment in emergency preparedness is tremendous.

National policy, foreign aid, stockpile and inventory issues, and bioterrorism responses require a robust public health infrastructure. The United States has a weak record in sustaining long-term investments in public health infrastructure. It might be appropriate for academic health center leaders to talk to the American public about the importance of long-term maintenance of investments in public health. There has been a very successful effort in getting the nation to focus on research and development (R&D). A similar effort in the field of public health could lay a foundation for keeping new drug research and development on target for a number of generations. The solutions are going to be found in systems and not silos, and academic health centers need to decide how to facilitate the creation of systems that work for people in times of emergency.

Chapter Six

Leadership in Security, Terrorism, and City Management

Lew Stringer Jr., MD

I t is only for the last two years that joint accreditation by the Joint Commission on Accreditation of Healthcare Organizations (JCAHO) has required a hospital to have emergency management procedures and an understanding of how the hospital fits into local, all-risk disaster planning. Indeed, emergency management is something new to the health care industry. However, recent events have made disaster planning critical. Unfortunately, the health care industry often is not even mentioned in such planning, and has much to do to increase preparedness levels, including readiness to surge. This paper presents some of the issues involved in disaster planning and describes what is happening in North Carolina.

The Major Issue: How to Surge

If we wait for a disaster to happen, it will be too late. Each community needs a medical emergency plan that has been put together by the people who are going to provide the emergency services. The plan should cover planning, training, and response, with 99 percent of the plan involving planning and training before any response is needed.

Before September 11, it was difficult to include health care in disaster planning. North Carolina has been holding classes in weapons of mass destruction (WMD) for health care providers and other emergency service agencies since 1998, but fewer than fifteen doctors from the whole state would attend. Since September, more than 500 physicians have come to the eight-hour class.

North Carolina, the tenth most populated state, has received $23 million from the Department of Health and Human Services (HHS) for disaster planning. Of this amount, $3.3 million was spent on hospital planning and preparedness—not much money when divided by the number of hospitals in the state. (There is currently a bill before Congress, the Public Health Threats and Emergencies Act sponsored by Senators Ted Kennedy (D-Mass.) and Bill Frist (R-Tenn.) that would appropriate more funding for state and local planning in the health care community.)

In 1996, Congress passed a law requiring police, fire departments, emergency medical services (EMS), health departments, hospitals, and the health care community to get together on a regular basis to plan for dealing with hazardous materials effectively. This is what we need for disaster planning, too.

Included in disaster planning should be representatives from every aspect of health care, for example, the medical society, which could work with retired doctors and nurses. Another group to include are veterinarians because zoonotic diseases are a significant problem in terms of disaster. Every group's efforts must be coordinated now rather than later. When a catastrophe occurs, part of the disaster can be the inability to utilize all the donated goods and unsolicited, uncoordinated volunteers who pour in to help.

When Hurricane Allison struck, not one of the fifty-one hospitals in the community one knew the others' disaster plans. After they had lost 1,700 beds and 75 percent of the intensive care units (ICUs), and 75 percent of the emergency departments (EDs) were going to be out of service for some time, it took six days for the CEOs of all the hospitals to get together and decide what to do. Each hospital needs its own plan, but each one also needs to determine how it will fit in with everyone else.

Every community needs a local disaster medical system, too. What happens when a hospital emergency department is at four times the normal capacity during the winter and then surges to eight times the capacity? How will all the institutions in the area be aware of that situation? Can they help each other in a crisis, and help at another facility? If a standard disaster exercise that works for one and a half hours with everybody participating is a miracle, what happens if the emergency is for seventy-two hours? Five-plus days? Who will relieve those on duty?

What triage system is a hospital using? What type of disaster tag? If ten counties are bringing patients to one hospital, do the tags look similar? (Triage tags are not used in the majority of disasters because they are not used on a regular basis.) Is there a regional medical disaster-response system or plan? No city can take care of itself, except possibly Los Angeles and New York. We all depend on each other.

Is there a state plan, with every aspect of preparedness included in the planning? How many medical beds are available? Are they all licensed? The Veterans Administration and the Department of Defense, which probably have many beds, probably do not have much staff. Where would the personnel come from to care for disaster victims if we did find empty beds?

A Federal Plan for a Potential Smallpox Attack

The draft plan for smallpox written by the Centers for Disease Control and Prevention (CDC) is too academic. We must be able to find x number of facilities that had high-efficiency particle-arresting (HEPA) filters on the exhalation of the buildings or were 100 yards from any occupied dwelling? Or, if a facility is taken on a quarantine basis, who would it go back to? Would they take it back? There is good material in the draft, but a lot of issues still need study. How many beds are available? Burn beds? Ventilators? How will they be tracked? What can be done if 1,700 more hospital beds need to be staffed? It is possible that not even a few states could handle such a situation.

A Three-Tiered Emergency Response System

With the $11.5 million North Carolina has received from the Department of Justice, the state is establishing some medical capabilities to call on in the event of a disaster. We have collaborated with the Special Operations Response Team, a nonprofit health group; the state health department; the Federal Emergency Medical System (EMS); and the state's Division of Emergency Management for work with eighty-six health departments covering the 100 counties in North Carolina. Some hospitals cannot handle even one contaminated patient, and three contaminated patients would close the emergency room. Now there will be ninety local facilities that can do triage and decontamination. They will be encouraged to include health-care staff from the health department and emergency rooms so that they can be up and doing something within thirty minutes. (They have to be willing to leave that county to go to another county to provide mutual aid.)

North Carolina has seven Level 1 trauma systems, made up of sister hospitals in a county, who talk to each other on a regular basis. Now, instead of each hospital reinventing the wheel, there will be one system, based primarily in Centers for Excellence and medical schools. Toward this end, the state received an additional $40,000 to do planning and bring in the sister hospitals, the county health directors, and the medical societies. The hospitals are looking at where they are, how many beds they have, and what they have in assets. In this way, they can decide what is needed and develop a plan for handling surge capacity per region, for example, how to handle bed-regulating (i.e., transferring and moving patients around) and how they would report to the state so that the seven Level 1 trauma systems are plugged into what is happening.

The hospitals have also been asked to form regional medical teams through the trauma center. Each team would include one or two people from each hospital (so that no one would be overloaded), including a doctor, nurses, a pharmacist, the county health director, and the regional veterinarian. Each region would have an emergency public information team of four people supported by the Federal government through state health departments. An environmental health and epidemiology expert and a case investigator will also be on board in each region, as will a hazardous material team.

The Governor is responsible for any declared crisis within the state of North Carolina. The health department is the lead agency, determining where the problem is and the teams that have to go fix it. At the state level, emergency management could know all the state, regional, and local assets that could be brought to bear on the situation, and help the hospitals manage the situation.

At the state level, there are 2,800 equipped and trained law enforcement officers and a health bioterrorist response team. We hope to do this over a three-year period, spending $11.5 million. The effort was started before Secretary Thompson announced his bioterrorist initiative; fortunately both North Carolina and the secretary's initiative are the same, i.e., both call for all state agencies to be coordinated.

What can a Type 1 team do? It can go out and set up an austere medical environment. It can manage the national pharmaceutical stockpile; handle drug distribution and immunizations; provide decontamination services for up to 200 ambulatory patients; provide mental health services and preventive medicines; and handle mass fatalities. It could deploy teams made up of all types of health care providers for seven or more days, maintaining the standards of the national disaster medical system. At regional areas, the trauma system should be responsible for responding within the region within six hours; if moved elsewhere in the state, they should be able to respond within twenty-four hours. They could work in hospitals and establish alternate care facilities. Their duration of service would be a maximum of three days. Then they could be rotated from the other seven regions, all rotated again, again trying to get buy-in from all the health care community.

The Type 3 teams would have to be operational more quickly than the Type 1 team because the Type 3 teams are on the street, go to a hospital to help out or, if needed, go to somewhere else in the state within two hours. They would not be asked to go out of their county or local community for more than three days in a row without rotation. The Federal government has a plan, the Emergency Support Function 8 (ESF8), that includes all health and medical personnel across the nation. Its Health Alert Network will become an excellent way to tie all the components together. It will be electronic- as well as fax-capable. When fully set up, the system will alert local personnel to look at the new information being sent.

Conclusion

Whatever you do, do something. Put together a response that will work. Start at the local level, work to the regional level, and then to the state level, and also tie into the Federal system. The health care industry must be considered a first-responder. Hospitals and the health care industry must be included in disaster planning because they are in a crisis mode on a day-to-day basis.

California has devised the hospital instant command system (ICS), which works well. If every hospital works under one system, the state and Federal governments, and the medical schools and hospitals, would understand what to do. They would know when nurses and doctors rotate from one hospital to another or transfer to a hospital in another city. We wouldn't have to reinvent the wheel again and again.

Communications are vital to the entire enterprise. Remember, however, that the most difficult communications system to set up is getting everybody to sit down on a regular basis and work together. Until this happens, nothing will work.

Chapter Seven

Military Education and Practice Models

James A. Zimble, MD

I n this paper, I provide a brief look at the history of the Uniformed Services University of the Health Sciences (USU). I also explain how the work of the university not only fills military needs, but also has ramifications in civilian life. Indeed, its mission statement declares, in part, that the Uniformed Services University is devoted to "learning to care for those in harm's way." The "learning" is directed not only at students, but also at faculty and researchers and is today particularly relevant to learning how to take care of people in harm's way as a result of terrorist activities.

University History

In 1972, the U.S. government ended both the draft and an unpopular war. The military faced a shortage of physicians, and the Armed Forces Physicians' Appointment and Residency Consideration Program (Berry Plan) was about to end. The Berry Plan allowed all physicians who were liable for active military duty to volunteer for a Reserve commission and go in the service at a mutually acceptable time. At about the same time, Congressman Edwin Edwards (D-La.), who had been trying to establish a school of medicine for military personnel since the end of World War II, became chairman of the Appropriations Committee of the U.S. House of Representatives. Thus, the Uniformed Services University of the Health Sciences was born in 1972.

NOTE: Any opinion expressed by the author does not necessarily reflect the view of the U.S. Department of Defense.

The first class of twenty-nine students graduated in 1980. The university now has a class of 165 in the school of medicine and more than 3,100 graduates. They represent a little more than one-fifth of physicians on active duty in the Army, Navy, and Air Force. USU also trains officers in the U.S. Public Health Service. There are about 300 faculty on campus; about one-half are in the basic sciences. They are primarily civilians.

Teaching Methods

USU focuses its teaching in three major areas: character-building, medical skills, and military skills. Teaching a combination of professional character-building and military skills is called "officership." The university wants to make sure that its graduates understand that they are military officers. The teaching of ethical principles used in medicine is called "physicianship." The teaching of military skills and medical skills together is called "operational medicine." Thus, the university produces graduates who can practice medicine in a military environment, can practice military medicine with all its unique requirements, and are military medical officers.

Retention in the Military

The military needs physicians to remain in service. In this regard, USU has one advantage over other medical schools: Its students do not pay tuition; instead, students make a seven-year commitment to the military beyond graduation, becoming career physicians in the military. By the time they have paid back their obligations, they are so close to retirement that they stay on until retirement. Approximately 93 percent of physicians who have graduated from the university are still on active duty. No other institution has such a record of staying power, although much of it is obligated staying power.

Military Medicine

The military needs physicians and other medical personnel who can hit the ground running; therefore, during the course of their four years of study, students master a significant amount of subject matter unique to the military.

The military physician curriculum is taught for approximately 174 weeks in the school of medicine; other USU schools study the curriculum for about 150 weeks. The school also requires about 750 more contact hours than is normally required in a school of medicine. In addition, a graduate school of nursing provides a master's degree for the advanced practice nurse in family nursing practice and in nurse anesthesia. Both courses incorporate the readiness and military uniqueness issues, along with the various subject matters required for understanding population health community medicine. In 2003, the university will begin a third advanced practice course in clinical nurse specialists for perioperative nurses; they are in great demand in the military. There are only 30 students in each class, but 123 students have graduated, and 118 are still serving. Thus, there is a career field for nurses as well as for physicians at USU.

There are also several interdisciplinary programs. The utility of the course in emerging infectious diseases has become quite apparent today. Affiliations with twenty military treatment facilities allow for rotations around the country. We also have affiliations with overseas Army and Navy laboratories that belong to the Department of Defense and these sites are resources for our programs as are eight Centers of Excellence, and two institutes. The military curriculum includes field operations. Between their first and second year, students are sent to the U.S. Marine Base at Quantico, Virginia, where they become accustomed to the field.

In their fourth year, students participate in graded exercises at Fort Sam Houston, getting a great deal of hands-on skill experience in dealing with weapons of mass destruction and performing in leadership roles. They earn their Advanced Cardiac Life Support (ACLS) and Advanced Trauma Life Support (ATLS) certifications while there.

Continuing Education

USU delivers a continuing education curriculum, similar to the one for graduate medical education. The university assembles panels of specialists with military experience so that, within the curriculum of their various specialty programs, continuing education students can receive information directly related to the unique military aspects of their discipline. Subjects include combat casualty care, epidemiology, health promotion, disease prevention, and accident prevention.

The Department of Preventive Medicine is larger than those in many schools of public health. Most schools of medicine have about 13 contact hours in the field of tropical medicine and hygiene. USU has 130 contact hours because that is where the troops go. The physicians who graduate from the school have an absolute commitment to keeping troops from becoming patients, rather than waiting until there are patients to be taken care of. One field exercise, for example, is in chemical, biologic, radiologic, and nuclear and high explosives (CBRNE).

The Combat Casualty Care Research Center in the Department of Military and Emergency Medicine teaches a number of courses to people outside the military. Students include law enforcement agents and first-responders around the country. The program was launched with counter-narcotic money that came to the Department of Defense and was originally used primarily for the U.S. Park Police in Washington, D.C., the U.S. Marshals Service, the Federal Bureau of Investigation, staff at the Department of the Treasury, county and state police, and emergency medical teams (EMTs). Well over 5,000 civilians have been trained in short courses, including courses that train the trainers. To date, the information has gone out to at least 750 government and other agencies in just about every state through distance-learning techniques and teams sent out to sites. The Armed Forces Radiobiologic Institute (AFRI), which became part of the university in 1993, was instrumental in creating the dose curves for anthrax spores needed to decide exactly what dosages the U.S. Postal Service needed to make certain sterile letters were being delivered after the anthrax episode in Fall 2001. It is a unique national resource. A calibrated nuclear reactor capable of pulsing as an atomic detonation can deliver calibrated fast and slow neutron curves to large animal-exposure rooms. It enables researchers to study what is necessary for radiologic defense and radiation protection, and for treating radiologic casualties and protecting rescue workers. A course in the medical effects of ionizing radiation (MEIR) has been offered for about forty years. Today, it is available through distance learning and also teams that go to various sites to teach. There is no other program like this in the United States, and it has a definite impact on what we worry about in relation to homeland defense and homeland security.

Utilizing a linear accelerator, probably the largest cobalt source east of the Mississippi, investigators are doing radio protectant research with depleted uranium, finding those particular pharmaceuticals that will actually allow for enhanced exposure and cleanup operations and for biodosimetry. They have also developed ways of looking at DNA breakage within the cells to be able to determine fairly accurately the radiation dose to which a victim may have been exposed.

Another course in the Department of Military Medicine covers Civilian Disaster and Humanitarian Assistance Medicine (CDHAM). Many people assume that any physician or family nurse practitioner is capable of going into any situation and able to perform effectively. The military, for example, has been guilty of deploying pediatricians into disaster areas when they have had absolutely no exposure to the level of poverty, malnutrition, and disease-impact that are endemic in these situations. We teach courses to the specialists in the school of medicine so that they can be competent and helpful in disaster situations.

Partnerships with other organizations are critical to the university's mission. For example, Department of State employees worldwide come at least twice a year to the university campus in Bethesda, Maryland, for their continuing medical education. Other partners are the National Aeronautics and Space Administration (NASA); the Veterans Administration (VA); and the Departments of Justice, Education, and Health and Human Services.

When USU was asked to develop a course in the basics of weapons of mass destruction and bioterrorism that could be disseminated rapidly, the university decided the best way to go was to partner with a commercial enterprise—Lippincott, Williams, and Wilkins. The result is a ten-module course (now in beta testing) consisting of about twelve hours of asynchronous, self-paced course work. A demonstration is available on the Internet at <www.wmddemo.com>. Subject areas include the identification of CBRN devices, threat evaluation, response planning, the role of quarantine, the psychological effects of WMD, and principles of decontamination. The most important and relevant element of the course is that the registrants are entered into a database. The database's registrar and reporting function lists who has had the training and when. It is vital to understanding who is prepared to follow up with any disaster plan.

Conclusion

USU works constantly to stay up to date with what is happening in the world today. It makes a point of teaching how to practice good medicine in bad places, *bona loces malas*. Military medicine is unique, but it also has elements that can be translated to other academic health centers throughout the country. USU is a national resource with information and expertise that should be shared with myriad organizations and institutions.

Chapter Eight

Tapping the Power of Health in Foreign Policy

Ambassador Robert E. Hunter, PhD
C. Ross Anthony, PhD

CHANGING CONCEPTS OF SECURITY

Ambassador Hunter

In many respects, what happened on the 11th of September in New York City, Washington, D.C., and just outside Shanksville, Pennsylvania, is similar to what happened at Pearl Harbor. Each event was not just a sneak attack and a blow to our psyche enveloped in tragedy. Both events also had a defining impact on our understanding of America's role in the world.

The Japanese attack on Pearl Harbor in 1941 ended the U.S. sense of isolation. Later, the Cold War had the same effect. With the end of that war, Americans for a time regained the feeling of sanctuary afforded by two broad oceans. But with the World Trade Center attack and subsequent anthrax scare, we Americans lost, or at least we should have lost, our sense of insulation—a sense that somehow, the United States, a special country, would be immune from what was happening to other countries. This belief was more perception than reality.

In this paper, I describe some of the reasons for changing attitudes and foreign policy initiatives in the United States since the end of the Cold War. I also discuss the new roles that health and the health professions should play in domestic and foreign policy as a result of September 11, and the contribution that increased U.S. engagement abroad, including foreign aid, can make in the service of fighting terrorism and otherwise promote America's key goals in the world.

Paradigms for Foreign Policy

In retrospect, the Cold War was a relatively simple time that Americans thought would last forever. We missed the underlying trends because of the compelling quality of the foreign policy framework that defined the Cold War. That framework could be reduced to three statements: (1) contain the Soviet Union and its allies and acolytes; (2) confound communism; and (3) lead a growing, global economy. The last-named role was played, in part, to provide the wherewithal for winning the Cold War. If anything interfered with these paradigms in American foreign policy, the leadership of this nation, for good and sufficient reason, would play it down.

The health professions had a significant although ancillary role to play during this time, particularly in the area of public health abroad. The role emanated from talk about healthy societies in Western Europe and elsewhere that came out of the Marshall Plan and continued afterward. The medical profession's other, secondary role was as part of "the battle for hearts and minds," a term used quite a bit in Vietnam but which also had a broader application: How could the United States compete with Communism to show that its way of life is superior?

The Cold War came to an end when ideas and economics proved to be more powerful than military arms. The world saw not only the collapse of the Soviet Union, but also a fundamental transformation of all countries in the Soviet bloc. In fact, this was the most profound strategic retreat in all of peacetime history; what happened to the Soviet Union was unprecedented in history. Mr. Gorbachev started out with his glasnost (openness) and his perestroika (transformation) to save communism and the Soviet Union. However, the power of what he unleashed—in terms of people looking at how they wanted to conduct their lives and provide for their families and societies—overwhelmed what had been the most potent empire from at least the beginning of the twentieth century. One of the effects was that it left the United States without its first two paradigms.

Only the idea of leading a growing global economy remained, and it has led many Americans to believe that there was a true peace dividend. The dividend was not so much financial as an ability to retreat from the outside world, for two reasons. First, with the collapse of the Soviet Union and the end of the nuclear balance of terror, the United States found itself less threatened by the outside world than at any time since Pearl Harbor. Second, the United States emerged from the Cold War with a stunning amount of national and international power.

During the last several years, in terms of incipient power, the United States has brought together unparalleled military power. We spend more money on defense than the next eleven countries in the world combined and more than twice as much as all the North Atlantic Treaty Organization (NATO) allies. No conventional military power on earth can take on the United States.

Economically, the United States is first among equals. The European Union (EU) has about 80 percent of the American gross national product, but it comprises 360 million people compared to America's 280 million, and it does not have our single, integrated economy. Politically and culturally, the United States also is very much in the lead internationally. Indeed, all told, we have an extraordinary degree of incipient power, probably more than any other country, empire, or group of countries has had since the collapse of the Roman Empire.

Yet despite all this power and relatively few threats, the United States soon discovered that the very processes that helped bring the Cold War to an end and led to our country's position in the world were also leading ineluctably to its becoming ever-more deeply and permanently engaged abroad. Every single profession now knows the impact of globalization. It has thrust the American people deeply into the outside world, far more than we might like and far beyond what we have any power to control.

Redefining Security

In the making of American foreign policy, the country is witnessing a new definition of security. It goes beyond the definition, prevalent during the Cold War, which was dominated by the military power so essential to containing the Soviet Union. The new definition marks the return of the other elements of the great triad of power: military, economic, and diplomatic. Furthermore, other countries are coming to understand that the United States government actually controls a far smaller proportion of its foreign policy than it did in the past. A much greater portion is controlled by the private sector, in particular by international corporations. Major elements of the American economy are firmly rooted in the outside world, having an impact on the U.S. economy as well as on other economies—in particular, those of the European Union.

In addition, the role of nongovernmental organizations (NGOs) has become increasingly important as part of U.S. foreign policy. In the last ten years, much, if not most, of the new thinking about roles and responsibilities of governments and institutions has come not from the U.S. government but from NGOs.

Thus, even before September 11, there was a progressive understanding of how the world will not leave us alone.

The Health Professions: Front and Center

The health professions, rather than being of secondary importance in American foreign policy, henceforth will be right at the center, for a variety of reasons. One reason is that bioterrorism will help define how we deal with a new phenomenon called "asymmetrical warfare." When countries lack conventional power but still want to confound the United States, some of them reach for terrorism and weapons of mass destruction that can be developed and used without the full panoply of a major industrial economy or other instruments of sizeable power. The tactics of asymmetrical war are not designed to neutralize American power; they cannot do that. But they try to counter it in particular ways. Bioterrorism thus poses a potential new threat to the U.S. homeland. In this regard, the U.S. health community will be called upon to play a major role in the nation's defense, especially in what is called "consequence management."

Another reason that health and the health professions will play increased roles in domestic and foreign policy is that diseases coming to the United States, including drug-resistant diseases, now have a far greater prevalence and proliferation in this country than in the past. For example, northern Virginia has been facing a near crisis from drug-resistant tuberculosis brought to this country by immigrants, including from the former Soviet Union. Similarly, in many parts of the world, Americans and others cannot travel, or at least cannot travel safely, because of the rise of disease and other health-related challenges, with HIV/AIDS being only the best known. Furthermore, countries facing health crises are less likely to be political and socially stable and economically productive; and some of them are prone to become hotbeds for conflict and terrorism. Dr. Anthony discusses these points more fully in the paper that follows.

The Advantages of Promoting Development— Especially Health

Throughout the world, however, especially since the end of the Cold War, the United States has withdrawn from its deep engagement in the development process. In terms of official development aid (ODA), the United States ranks lowest, as a percentage of gross national product (GNP), among all industrial countries. True, President Bush now understands that foreign aid has certain advantages, and he will raise American foreign aid spending by $10 billion to a total of $15 billion a year after three years. However, the United States will still be falling far short of both what we can do and what we need to do to promote our own interests, as well as those of peoples in societies left behind by the economic advance of recent years. Without major changes in the way in which they experience the global economy, they will be left behind by globalization as well.

The good news is that the American health community has tremendous opportunities to make a difference. Its health and health-care professions have an increasingly important role to play in U.S. foreign policy and national security in two senses. First, directly, they and counterparts in the European Union and elsewhere can do things of a practical nature, including dealing with health challenges abroad that will help in dealing with security threats. Second, indirectly, the U.S. health community can also "do well by doing good," in helping to foster, for legitimate reasons, a far better reputation for the United States in many parts of the world than, regrettably, it has today. This would be a demonstration of the positive values for which America stands and the vast contribution that we have made and will continue to make in promoting the well-being of others. No area is more important than health and health care in getting across this message of help and of hope.

Many developing countries face declines in productivity, loss of income, decreases in life span, and a series of other problems that, in addition to their economic consequences, are helping to spawn crises and terrorism. If the United States is to deal with terrorism in the long term, it cannot just look at the effects of crises. It must also look at the causes. These are not the ones that lead an Osama Bin Laden and his people to do what they did: There can be no adequate explanation for such criminal behavior. Rather, to borrow a term from Mao Tse-tung, counter-terrorism strategy has to include dealing with "the sea within which" the terrorists "swim." That means dealing with the circumstances that lead people in other countries to be supportive, or at least tolerant, of terrorism. Much of it has to do with poverty, lack of development, lack of education, and, yes, poor health and poor health care. The struggle for hearts and minds, in effect, is no longer a secondary matter; it is something that has to be absolutely on the front burner of U.S. national security policy

Conclusion

The central lesson of the current age, the age of globalization and American power, is that if the United States is to shape a world in which we would like to live, we have to find a way to turn power into lasting influence. The way to do this is to create attitudes, institutions, practices, and policies that work for this country because they also work for others. The United States, if it is to succeed, must succeed as part of a broader international society, and the health professions are right there on the point.

HEALTH AS FOREIGN POLICY

Dr. Anthony

I n an era characterized by rapid globalization and an absence of critical challenge comparable to the Cold War, but a rising threat of terrorism, the traditional view of national security and how best to formulate foreign policy in this new world paradigm is changing rapidly. Traditionally, health has been viewed at best as a second-order consideration in U.S. foreign policy, which concentrated instead on military and economic power.

Convincing health practitioners and researchers that health is important to foreign policy is relatively easy, but, on the other hand, convincing foreign policy decision makers that health can be an important policy tool has proven to be quite difficult. In fact, if U.S. foreign policy responds to terrorism with military intervention alone, without attacking its root causes, it is likely the U.S. government will spend billions of dollars trying to prevent future catastrophes without changing the environment from which they come. We must turn our attention also to the roots of terrorism and means to change that environment. Health is one such policy intervention.

Building on the previous paper by Dr. Hunter dealing with the changing nature of security, this paper models why health is a powerful policy tool for achieving foreign policy objectives and then examines how policy might be organized to be an effective policy lever.

Health: A Powerful Foreign Policy Instrument

Health is a powerful instrument of international engagement because it has powerful synergistic effects on many aspects of development and individual freedom, as well as on international trade, technology, and infectious disease- flows. These interactions can be illustrated in two interconnected models: one domestic and one global.

The first looks at the effects of a health policy intervention on the domestic environment of a target country. For instance, consider a U.S. aid initiative designed to improve a country's public health system. The intervention will have direct impact on income (public health workers receive wages) and on health status. With the improvement in health status, days lost from work will decrease as illness decreases, and worker productivity will increase as human capital increases, all leading to greater per capita incomes and greater development.

These changes are also closely linked with education and a number of other variables. If income per capita goes up, malnutrition among children will go down, as will infant mortality. As families come to believe that their children will live to maturity, fertility and population growth rates fall further after a time lag, increasing income per capita. Education, particularly of women, is critical. Improved nutrition of the young improves ability to learn. And as countries develop and women become better educated, the women take a more active role in the economy. In a synergistic way, better-educated women are key to the health status of families, particularly of children, and to growing economies. All of these factors work together to spur development.

From the foreign policy perspective, the most important aspect of this first model may be that all the factors—better health, higher income, more education, and changing population variables—are likely to lead to more stable societies. Such societies are more likely to be democratic, peace-loving, socially tolerant, and valued partners in the international community.

Turning to a simple global model, one can trace feedback loops to all countries. From a health perspective, an infectious disease such as tuberculosis can flow from a target country to the United States, transmitted by somebody immigrating to the United States or an American tourist's exposure in another country. Spread of disease to the United States population need not come directly from the country of origin. There are secondary flows, or feedback loops, that end up affecting the U.S. population.

For example, someone may be infected with the Ebola virus and travel to Canada; then, from Canada, the virus is transmitted to the United States. Infectious diseases flow back and forth in a dynamic equilibrium at any point in time, but that equilibrium can change dramatically at any time, for example, either positively by a new vaccine or negatively by say bioterrorism.

Health is closely linked not only to local economic prosperity and stability, but also to the global economy. A health initiative that improves the economy of a developing country will result in greater trade opportunities for the United States, as imports of American products increase. Even if the importing country demands goods from another country, one would expect demand for U.S. products to increase as those countries look to the United States to fill their need for intermediate goods or use some of their increased income to buy American products. As a matter of fact, demand might circulate back, with the developing country asking for even more imports from the United States. In an interrelated global economy, economic activity stimulates production and trade in all countries. As pointed out by others, this process is not free of problems. Economic activity and trade must be subject to rules to insure fair competition and oversight to prevent environmental degradation and other problems.

There are further economic and cultural advantages. A disease-free environment is a prerequisite for trade and tourism. Globalization also brings a tremendous amount of technology transfer, which increases the speed of development and coincidentally increases demand for high technology products, including health, related goods such as pharmaceuticals for which the United States is a leading producer. Economic development, stability around the world, more positive attitudes toward the United States, and an environment critical of terrorism are all closely related to the health of the world community.

In today's policy world, policy makers demand evidence of positive effects. Unfortunately health's policy strength—strong multisector effects—can also be its weakness. The multiple effects and flows of health initiatives are difficult to quantify, tease out, and prove, particularly to the foreign policy community which wants to see clear ways to intervene and bring about change. In fact, almost all of the research and information needed to make the case for health intervention as a good foreign policy tool and to quantify that effect are missing.

Using Health as a Tool of Foreign Policy

Health can serve as a powerful foreign policy tool to deal with some of the root causes of terrorism and the deteriorating image of America around the world. In addition to the multidimensional effects outlined above is the fact that health is shared human value. No one wants to see a child in pain or a mother lose a child—everyone can identify with these situations regardless of race, religion, or politics. Health is one policy instrument that is neutral to factors like race, religion, and politics that make it so hard for people to get along, understand, and work with each other. It is for exactly these reasons that health is an extraordinarily powerful tool of engagement that can be used in all countries and across a broad spectrum of income levels.

Amartya Sen, the Nobel prizewinner who wrote *Development as Freedom,** encourages us to think about development not in terms of increases in per capita income but in terms of personal and societal freedoms. Such thinking would avoid the issue of distribution of income that often leads to situations found in many countries where economies are developing yet women and other minorities are left behind economically and socially. Development is a critical factor that affects all the other factors critical to freedom.

There are a number of different feasible approaches are available to guide the use of health as a foreign policy instrument, including concentrating on (1) control of the spread of infectious disease to the United States, (2) economic development, (3) foreign country stability, (4) host country personal and national freedom, and (5) U.S. global image. Each approach targets a different outcome, and, although the approaches are not contradictory, they lead to different policy prescriptions. A few of these approaches are examined briefly below.

First, one could target a reduction of the threat of infectious diseases imported into the United States. To reduce the threat to U.S. citizens of disease brought to the United States by both U.S. citizens and foreigners, policymakers would probably concentrate on such dangers as bioweapons, HIV/AIDS, tuberculosis (particularly drug-resistant TB), and Ebola. They could construct a matrix to determine the effects of each disease and analyze which one would have the greatest impact and then target each dis-

---

* Sen, Amartya. 1999. *Development as Freedom.* Oxford: Oxford University Press.

ease accordingly. Such an approach might also lead to a greater emphasis on testing at borders and stricter visa requirements.

Another option might concentratng on enhancing foreign country stability. The objective would again lead one to look at HIV/AIDS, which has a tremendous effect within countries, particularly with regard to infant mortality, and affects the total socioeconomic structure, including the number of orphans. However, unlike policy that emphasizes curtailing the spread of disease to the United States, this objective would likely see initiatives designed to spur economic development and provide basic health care services to local people. The United States could, as Sen recommends, look at aspects of health care that have the greatest effect on personal and national freedoms; the result would likely include many of the policy proposals above, but would also include actions to advance education and democratic pluralism.

Still another option would be to concentrate on health initiatives abroad that have the greatest impact on the U.S. global image. In health care, approach would likely emphasize health care services, including basic public health primary care, for the largest number of people, including the poor and disadvantaged. These actions could include sharing intellectual property rights for pharmaceuticals or provision of HIV drugs, as well as partnerships with American health care professionals. They might also include actions such as high visibility curative campaigns in areas like eye surgery or helping the victims of land mines that are high visibility activities that generally do not change the basic health status of countries.

None of these approaches is necessarily right or wrong and as indicated may overlap. Also, researchers would need to evaluate each approach and the advantages and disadvantages of each, in order to help guide U.S. foreign policy. Foreign policy objectives change over time, and health used as an instrument of foreign policy would also need to adapt. Given the lack of information and many unanswered questions, policymakers do not really know how to go forward or set priorities. Not only do we not know the with confidence the effects of each intervention;we do not even know what infrastructure is needed to be effective in all of the health interventions that might be considered. With the present information, it is difficult to compare health initiatives to traditional foreign policy interventions and determine which are more effective. There are more questions than answers, and also a lack of the type of analysis and information needed to make good foreign policy.

HIV in South Africa: A Case Study in Foreign Policy

The problem of HIV/AIDS in southern Africa is well-known and well-docu-mented. Nevertheless, the sheer breadth of human pain and suffering is dif-ficult to comprehend. In South Africa, for example, 4.7 million people in the year 2000, are living with HIV and 420,000 of these have full-blown AIDS. There are 100,000 deaths from AIDS in South Africa per year. By 2010, life expectancy is expected to drop to about 40 years, and two million children will be orphans. Infection rates are presently projected to reach 16% by 2006.

If we look at the HIV crisis in South Africa from a foreign policy per-spective, a number of factors become important. The stability of the coun-try could be threatened. The economic costs to treat victims will be immense. Economic growth is slowing, worker productivity is falling, social unrest is growing, crime is rising, and even without extensive use of the new antiviral drugs, health care expenditures are over $500 million, a price tag South Africa can ill afford. All of this is likely to lead to social unrest. At the same time, the judicial and educational systems are being undermined because HIV/AIDS infection rates are higher among the better-off and better-educated, who have enough money to engage in the sex trade. In essence, South Africa is caught in a downward spiral of social and economic problems. At this time of great need, government response is reported to be weak.

Furthermore, HIV prevalence in the South African military and police is running at over 22 percent, undermining morale. This also limits South Africa's ability to maintain law and order and participate in regional peace-keeping operations. In addition, the military is highly mobile, and soldiers spread the disease easily and quickly. In terms of international security, South Africa is crucial to southern Africa's security, yet the nation's military will not able to deal with the situations they might be asked to handle.

From a foreign policy perspective, this is a crisis in the making, and that interventions not taken at the same time could have a critical impact and help avert not only a health disaster, but also a looming foreign policy prob-lem both for both the United States and South Africa. It is not by accident that much the world is starting to realize that there is an urgent need that affects us all from many perspectives.

A Role for Academic Health Centers

In this endeavor, there is a critical role for academic health centers. First, particularly as it relates to policy options, is the tremendous amount of research needs to be conducted to determine the effectiveness of health as a foreign policy intervention. If health can be made an important component of foreign policy—or deserves to be one—academic health centers should be on the cutting edge in conducting the basic research needed and providing that information to policy makers. Until this basic research is conducted, it is unlikely that foreign policy decision makers will incorporate health as an important policy determinant.

Second, it is important to publicize and expand models that work. For instance, the American International Health Alliance (AIHA) partnership model is an effective instrument that has been proved in many countries in Eastern Europe and the former Soviet Union. Some forty academic health centers have been actively engaged, in a program of doing good things through a voluntary partnering effort on a wide range of health care activities in the states of the former Soviet Union and Eastern Europe.

American public support for just wars is common. The United States is spending about $1 billion a month in Afghanistan, but foreign aid and other such activities have always been a hard sell. If the fight against terrorism in the developing world is to be successful, academic health centers and others are going to have to help prove health offers a mechanism of engagement for a better world then, and then be willing to participate in constructive engagement with countries overseas.

Third, academic health centers have tremendous political clout. Located in most states, many have access to Congressional senators and representatives in ways that others do not. Voices of the health professionals need to be heard as a positive force telling policymakers what can be done, instead of simply standing back and waiting to respond to the next crisis.

Finally, academic health centers can, and I would argue should, be leaders in the effort to spread good health practices around the world and use health engagement as a positive tool of U.S. foreign policy. If academic health centers which are on the forefront of technology and delivery, and include our brightest academic minds and most leaders of American medicine are not willing or capable of stepping forward at such a critical junction in history, who else can reasonably be expected to do so?

In response to September 11, RAND established the Center for Domestic and International Health Security. The center is looking at issues of domestic preparedness and response as well as international health as a mechanism for international engagement dealing with some of the root causes of terrorism, and for convincing policy leaders of the need to include health as a meaningful part of the foreign policy agenda.

Conclusion

The field of health care offers both an opportunity and a challenge to make a meaningful difference in the world today. Academic health centers have a special opportunity to make health an essential element of U.S. foreign policy because they can use their capabilities to do the needed research and provide the leadership. Presently, academic health centers are making a difference in terms of information, skills, and the development of partnerships with communities overseas. These efforts could be expanded.

If we are to succeed in our fight against terrorism, we have to develop strategies that enable us to change a situation that breeds it. Health can be a factor in that foreign policy strategy, but the changes required demand that foreign policy makers step outside their comfort zone.

Some 30 years ago, I set up and ran a community health project in the mountains of rural Nepal because I believed it was a means by which I could make a contribution that did not involve making political decisions that were not my right to make. Today, the same opportunity exists to use health care as a mechanism of human engagement. Our challenge is to turn the benefits of health care and the power of the United States into lasting influence and lasting change for a better world.

Chapter Nine

University Response to Terrorism: An Impressionistic Overview

Martin Michaelson, JD

> [It] seems the government had a true account of it, and several councils were held about ways to prevent its coming over. And people began to forget it [until] . . . Two men died of the plague at the upper end of Drury Lane.
>
> —*A Journal of the Plague Year*

I n this paper, I address not the content of an optimal academic medical center or university plan to manage terrorism-related risks. Rather, I comment on terrorism-related risk-management practices and tendencies of universities. In other words, it is like a lawyer addressing not so much what the prevailing law says but, instead, how it is being made.

The State of the Art

At universities, as elsewhere, terrorism-related risk-management comes under two main headings: prevention of, and reaction to, terrorism. Curiously, nearly all pertinent law and most university effort on the subject addresses prevention of terrorism. Very little of it, relatively speaking, addresses reaction or response to terrorist acts. Most universities, even the best, are severely unprepared to react effectively to a terrorist disaster of the first magnitude on campus. I would hazard to compare it with the unpreparedness nationally for a smallpox epidemic.

I recently sent an e-mail message to the general counsel of twenty-two leading universities around the country, all senior lawyers. The e-mail read:

> I seek to gauge the level of satisfaction or dissatisfaction of a sample of thoughtful university general counsels with their institutions' current terrorism-related crisis management policy.
>
> Your response to the following two-part question will be taken in confidence. . . . Do you consider (a) the institution's current policy to be approximately at the state of the art; and (b) [do you consider] the state of the art nationally of university planning for terrorism events to be generally satisfactory?

One remarkable outcome was that eighteen of the twenty-two general counsels did not respond at all to either part of the two-part question. Two of the four who did respond supplied their institution's crisis management plans, which they believed to be generally satisfactory but that, upon inspection, manifestly turned out to be far below the state of the art of crisis management. The two other institutions whose general counsel responded have so far done a somewhat better job of updating their crisis management plans, but neither of the universities is even arguably a prize winner in this category. Neither, for example, has a practical, coordinated administrative plan for decision-making in response to major disaster. Neither has an effective plan for evacuation of the campus.

Updating Crisis-Management Policies

Crisis management policies of universities throughout the country are in the process of revision. Some institutions have completed their revisions of these policies. Most have not. A review of most prevailing policies will show their gross inadequacy in preparing for institutional reaction to a major terrorist event.

One preeminent university's crisis-management plan identifies interruption of the institution's computers as the prime hazard at which the policy aims. Another university's policy amounts to little more than the assignment of specified personnel to be marshals in charge of various designated buildings on campus. A third institution's policy appears to have been written by a person who did not receive a college education; it consists of a series of elliptically expressed, hortatory bullet-points that fail to inform the reader about what to do in any event.

Most university crisis management-plan documents are not well written, comprehensive, or clear. Few such documents are even close to the quality that they would be if senior managers rather than middle managers had written them.

Probably no university in the United States at this point maintains an effective protocol for the physical relocation of all students, faculty, and staff in the event of a 4- or 8- or 16-hour notice of, for example, an explosion of a tactical nuclear device or the local occurrence of anthrax vapors of the type that closed the Hart Office Building of the U.S. Senate, among other buildings closed on Capitol Hill last Fall. Is there an academic medical center in this nation that could effectively treat 500 or 1,000 patients infected with any of the lethal so-called "select agents" (to use the terminology of the first legislated response to September 11, the USA Patriot Act)?

Much better, more sophisticated crisis-management regimes are beginning to emerge at several universities. But most of the institutions are far behind and show little inclination to surge forward. Their general counsels know that. Hence, the remarkably low response to my e-mailed questions.

It is not the purpose of this paper to address in depth why the response of universities to the risks of terrorism has been so relatively lackluster. Nor do I contend that, compared to other large organizations, universities have done worse so far. I do believe, however, that if the nation should have visited on it a second event or series of events on a scale of the September 11 events, a whole new level of commitment would follow in short order.

The Issue of Negligence

Does it make sense to wait for that to happen? How likely is a second catastrophe of that scale? What is the duty of care of universities in relation to that possibility? As fiduciaries, those in charge of universities have a duty, both ethical and legal, not to be negligent in relation to those for whom they are responsible. The paradigmatic definition of negligence in American law was offered by the great Judge Benjamin Cardozo in his 1928 opinion in *Palsgraf v. Long Island Railroad*. Every law student is taught this case. Its principle is the fundamental dictate of risk management theory.

Judge Cardozo essentially said that the duty of care is defined by multiplying the probability of an adverse event times the severity of the harm it would cause. Terrorism-related crisis management is an acute test of the validity of the Palsgraf paradigm. From an actuarial perspective—from the perspective of, say, united educators, the liability insurer of some 1,100 colleges and universities—the probability that any one college or university will suffer a major terrorist act is, to quote a senior united educators official, "miniscule." Yet the severity of such an event, by hypothesis, is more extreme than fire, flood, or earthquake. How does one reconcile and harmonize these extremes?

Yet, perhaps the probability of catastrophic terrorism on campus has been greatly underestimated. Graham Allison, former dean of the Kennedy School of Government at Harvard University and an authority on nuclear weapons, recently estimated the likelihood of a portable nuclear device being detonated in hostility in the coming decade in a civilian area to be greater than 50 percent. Considerable evidence indicates that a substantial number, certainly in the dozens and perhaps in the hundreds, of Russian-made portable nuclear weapons (the so-called "suitcase bombs") are unaccounted for. No responsible government authority knows where these atom bombs are. Are they in North America? Apparently we have no idea.

In Spring 2002, the *New York Times* broke the story that a Florida physician had last year treated one of the September 11 suicide terrorists for a case of what, in hindsight, is considered to have been anthrax. In its public statement about the matter, the FBI evinced an unconcern that seems astonishing. Yet, apparently without likely suspects in the matter, what else could the FBI say? Does Al Qaeda have anthrax capability? Apparently our government is unsure.

Universities, perhaps no less than government itself, have big disincentives to addressing clearly the risks of terrorism about which they know far too little and for which they have no adequate defenses. This may account. in part, for their suboptimal performance to date in terrorism-related crisis management.

Universities understandably seek to be perceived, especially by prospective students, as safe places, not as sandbag-covered bunkers. Paradoxically, a visible emphasis on terrorism-related crisis management (an initiative that should underscore institutional commitment to the personal safety of those who are there) seems to be perceived by at least some university presidents as underscoring vulnerability instead.

As a legal matter, the universities probably would not be found negligent in their campus plans for reaction to terrorism. Even if, abstractly speaking, an institution was negligent in this regard, it is hard, practically speaking, to conceive just how liability would attach. The issue is fundamentally not one of liability-avoidance, but rather one of wise institutional stewardship. The question devolves on whether current normative practice is wise. On that question, whatever its true answer, there has been scant debate at universities since September 11.

A Narrow View of Risk Management

We should be unsettled and concerned that, instead of devoting themselves to a rigorous planning for profound physical calamities and their aftermath, universities are devoting themselves to a narrower, albeit legitimate, set of issues in the realm of protecting their own more immediate interests in the conduct of research, the maintenance of positive and lawful relations with law enforcement authorities, and the like.

I recently conducted a program on terrorism-related issues with several colleagues. The more than 1,000 university in-house lawyers and other institutional officials participated expressed far less interest in crisis planning than in such prosaic, if increasingly complex, topics as how to comply with the Family Educational Rights and Privacy Act (FERPA), the student-records privacy law; and how to monitor legislative developments in the definition of chemical substances used in laboratories that the Federal government believes of potential interest to terrorists. Thus, higher education, on the whole, has succumbed to a tendency to treat the small, the familiar, the relatively manageable, and the analytically confined, while it has shrunk from grappling with the monstrous, the cataclysmic, the crippling, and the unknown. It has chosen the normal over the unprecedented, the relatively comfortable over the terrifying crisis.

A Broad View of Risk Management

History will judge, as it has always, whether that calculation (if it is a calculation and not mere inertia) was sound. We must acknowledge that if this judgment, this decision-fork, proves unsound, the verdict of history is likely to be harsh. One thinks of Churchill's postulated theme of the first volume of his monumental study of World War II, *The Gathering Storm*: "How the English-speaking peoples through their unwisdom, carelessness, and good nature allowed the wicked to rearm."

We should soberly consider whether future events will prove our current crisis-management efforts to be mere symbolic pacifiers of internal constituencies, an analogue to the civil defense plans of the early Cold War period, when schoolchildren were instructed to rest their heads on classroom desks in the event of nuclear attack. We should also consider whether the science establishment failed the nation when it passively accepted the withering away of smallpox vaccine stocks and judged civilian study of biological warfare to be politically incorrect or intellectually unimportant.

The contention here is not that universities, in the current environment of governmental unpreparedness for terrorism—an environment in which, according to a U.S. Department of Transportation study released in Spring 2002, 70 percent of knives went undetected at airport security checkpoints in recent weeks—could do an A-plus job of crisis management even if they set themselves to the task with zeal. I do believe that probably no university in the United States at present is as conscientiously devoted, at the highest levels of its governance, to these risks as to the risk of decline in its endowment.

Conclusion

In 1721, bubonic plague from Asia raced westward, decimating whole populations until it suspended for a time in Marseilles, France. Governments of northern European nations such as Holland and Britain placed relatively efficient total embargoes around their own ports to keep the infection out. There is some evidence that the British government, to rouse public concern, commissioned a journeyman author to write a tract that would well motivate the people of Britain to take due prophylaxis. To that end, he wrote a masterful book about an earlier, similar devastation, the bubonic plague of 1664–65 in London. His name was Daniel Defoe.

Many of the extraordinary leaders of academic health centers have talents in the field of public health and safety fully as impressive as Defoe's. Whether they now, or will soon, think that the risks of terrorism on campus warrant a rousing call to prepare and whether they will come forward on this momentous issue remains to be seen.

Chapter Ten

Crisis Information, Communications, and the Public

Maggie Fox

T he events of September 11 and the subsequent spate of anthrax illnesses left the American public feeling bewildered and unprepared
for terrorist attacks. This paper relates some lessons learned from
these events and suggests ways for academic health centers to work with
the media to keep the public better informed.

On September 11, I was on maternity leave from Reuters News Service
and in the backyard with my one-year-old. I live in Washington, D.C., about
five miles from the Pentagon, and my first thought was, What if one of the
airplanes had been carrying a big box of anthrax spores that were dispersed in the explosion? I took the baby inside and closed all the doors for
about ten minutes. Then I came to my senses. But this incident showed me
how little information is available to the public and how hard it is to quickly find out about local and national emergencies.

I also live about two blocks from the vice president's residence. When
the neighborhood found out Dick Cheney was in an undisclosed location,
we felt that if the neighborhood was not safe for Cheney, it was not safe for
us either. People did not like the implication that the vice president was
important and had to be protected but that we did not count.

This message from the government was not a good one, and it was
exacerbated when the public found out that President Bush had been flying around for several hours on September 11, evidently afraid or advised
not to touch down anywhere. People wanted leadership from a President

who would come back to Washington and say, "The American people cannot run from this, and I am not going to run from it either." That would have been a positive message.

For some time following the evening of September 11, the public did not get strong direction from the government. Luckily, government officials have admitted the mistakes they made, which has restored some trust. The lesson here is you must know what you are going to say about something before it happens. The people who did show leadership and have been held up as heroes are the police, the firefighters, the first-responders, and the hospital workers. It is hoped that organizations such as academic health centers can continue to bring this kind of leadership to whatever situation might prevail in the future.

Creating Public Trust

Tommy Thompson, secretary of the U.S. Department of Health and Human Services (HHS), has certainly learned some useful lessons about what not to do when trying to keep the public from panicking. When an anthrax case developed in South Florida, his first instinct, and maybe rightly, was to try to calm the public. Therefore, his first comment was that the affected man had been camping in North Carolina, and perhaps had contracted anthrax from a stream or some such place. That turned out not to be true, but his comment destroyed much of the trust that both the public and the media had in what the secretary had to say. He will have to go a bit farther to restore confidence. The media's fear is that Thompson's first instinct is going to be to suppress information to try to keep people calm. However, suppressing information does not calm people. The more information that is out there, the more people have to work with. People, in general, are reasonable and intelligent, and if they have the facts, they can handle extreme situations.

It is still difficult to get all the correct information out about the anthrax investigation. It is not entirely clear who is in charge. Is it the Federal Bureau of Investigation (FBI)? Is the U.S. Army Medical Research Institute of Infectious Diseases (USAMRIID) involved? The Centers for Disease Control and Prevention (CDC) still seems to be having trouble getting the necessary information. Admiral Ernie King, the Chief of Naval Operations during World War II, was once asked what the Navy's responsibility was in keeping the public and the media informed. His famous answer was, "Well, after the war's over, we should tell them who won." Sometimes the press feels that this is how the government treats them.

Getting Information to the Public

Perhaps academic health centers can fill this information gap for people. They are trusted sources with great resources, and could act as intermediaries between the government and the public. If something happens, it is going to be on the local level. If there is an outbreak of smallpox, it is going to be in Charlottesville or Norfolk or San Francisco, and it will probably be a local academic health center that gets the first case. The first reaction will probably be a bit of panic: "What do we tell people?"

My advice is to tell people what you know as soon as you know it. Have a plan to let people know things quickly, and explain what you are doing to find the answers. Suppose there is a report on local television that someone has shown up with pustules on his or her face that could be either chicken pox or smallpox. The test results may take forty-eight hours, but rather than sitting on the information, it would be better for the academic health center to call an immediate press conference and tell the media what it is doing to find out what this patient has. Such an event should be rehearsed ahead of time so that people know exactly what to say.

An easy way to disseminate information immediately to both the media and the public is through a Web site. You can reach the public and all the media immediately. (The Georgia Institute of Technology is conducting a survey of university Web sites to see what people find useful.) If you do not have answers, at least tell people your plan for dealing with the situation. Let people know what your resources are. Tell the public whether they should come to your emergency room. Such information can calm the media's panic and give reporters something to put in their stories. It also gives the public immediate access to information they need and that you want them to have.

Updating the Web site is important. We now have a 24-hour, 7-day news cycle. People no longer wait for the evening news or the morning paper. Most local TV stations will break into regular programming if they have a story that is even of moderate interest, let alone a bioterrorist attack. Thus, it is important to update a Web site as information is available and not build around some artificial news cycle.

Symptoms of anthrax are an example of information that can go on the Web site and be revised as new information becomes available. Unknown at first was the fact that anthrax was not just generalized flu-like symptoms: a cough or runny nose. This lack of information dearly cost a couple of postal workers who were told that they had flu when in fact they had anthrax. Erring on the side of caution will not create panic. Those postal workers did not panic. If anything, they were too calm. They went to the doctor and said they were postal workers and had certain symptoms. When they were told they had flu, they went home quietly and treated it as flu.

In addition, some of the postal workers at the Brentwood postal facility in Washington, D.C., did not opt for the vaccine. Some did not finish their full course of antibiotics. They trusted in their own ability to judge what might be wrong and what the risks might be, and, in fact, most of them were okay. There was some panic on Capitol Hill, but not as much as people might have feared. Buildings were closed, but that was a reaction by the government, not by the general public. People can deal with such a situation.

Before September 11, there had been worries about how Americans would handle an epidemic, especially if quarantine was necessary. Would people obey the quarantine? Would rescue workers seek to save their own families? Would teachers run home and leave the high school unstaffed? But a new atmosphere exists after September 11, a new feeling that people will deal with any situation that may arise. But that holds true only if people trust whoever is talking to them.

Establishing Relationships with the Media

Academic health centers are in a good position to create a feeling of trust with the media and, through the media, with the public. The center needs a centralized location during an emergency, for example, if a bioterrorist attack takes place, Dick Cheney shows up at the hospital with a heart attack, or the Governor falls and injures his head. If the media know they will get the latest information at this one location and no one else will scoop them, they will gather there, and the academic health center, in turn, will know where everybody is and will have an easy way to talk to them.

The media need to have the appropriate facilities at this location: seats, power points for people to plug in their computers, hookups for television, a couple of phone lines for people to feed, a way for the media, especially television, to do their feeds, and something to photograph every once in a while.

TV, and newspapers to some extent, will not do a story unless there is a picture to go with it. You do have to put somebody out there. It is also necessary to train spokespeople who are comfortable dealing with the media, with the issues, with knowing who to go to for fast answers. Donald A. Henderson, the director of the Office of Public Health Preparedness at HHS, is valued by anybody who covers bioterrorism because he knows what he is talking about and is comfortable with the media. He will take as much time as is needed and provide the necessary information for writing an accurate story that tells people what they need to know.

If there is no spokesperson, someone else is going to fill that gap, and it will likely be the local politicians. They see it as their job. Some just can't stop talking, but they do not always know what they are talking about. You do not want some city councilman to be the only source of information, giving out a lot of nonsense to the media. The media know this. Nonetheless, they cannot stop themselves either, and will report what these people say.

Many politicians were confused about anthrax on Capitol Hill. They bandied around phrases such as weapons-grade anthrax without knowing what it meant. Most of us in the media did not know what it meant either. As a result, much misinformation is still being repeated because reporters all feed on one another's reports. An academic health center can give information off the record if necessary, but it is important to make sure that whomever you are talking to understands what off-the-record means. Of course, the media love to quote people to prove that they have not made it up themselves. They do feel accountable to the public, and like to attribute information.

When briefing the media, it helps to have the relevant experts standing by, such as a doctor or firefighter. They will probably be busy, especially if there is something like a smallpox outbreak going on. However, as September 11 and the events of October have made clear, managing information is almost as important as managing the event itself. Dr. Henderson, Dr. Anthony Fauci of the National Institutes of Health (NIH), and former Surgeon General David Satcher are all examples of experts who are able to talk to the media.

Of course, doctors are reluctant to talk about cases in which they are not personally involved; if they are directly treating the patient, they cannot breach patient confidentiality. The way to resolve this dilemma is to get experts who can communicate with the public.

The media do not want to disseminate misinformation, but they all work under tense deadlines. It is better to have someone giving out the right information right away rather than have a reporter looking it up on the Internet. Some of the crazy stuff will get into their stories because they don't quite understand the subtle difference between one medical condition and another.

Some medical and other health professionals know how to speak in generalities about a medical condition. Make sure some of these experts are available when there is no specific information about an event. For instance, when President Bush choked on the pretzel, it was obvious there was not going to be much information from the White House, but I found out that Johns Hopkins University Hospital has a swallowing clinic with an expert who could talk about the vasovagal syncope, the fainting spell that can result from choking on something. In the end, it made an interesting story, even if it did not happen to President Bush.

One of the central precepts of journalism is called the so-what paragraph. So what? Why do we care about something? So what if someone in South Florida has anthrax? Could it be a bioterrorist attack? If it is naturally occurring anthrax, nobody is interested, but a bioterrorist attack is big news. We want the speculation because we want to know how important this issue is. Experts should fill that need with informed speculation or give good reasons why it could not be a bioterrorist attack. Help the media shoot down speculation.

Get to know the local media. When something happens, you will know whom you can trust and work with, and where the problem spots are going to be. For example, if there is a TV producer who will go with any rumor, you can troubleshoot before that happens. Form relationships now so that things will be manageable when trouble strikes. Some of the larger academic health centers are extremely good at this already.

You can get local media to do stories right now by talking to them about bioterrorism preparedness. Every media outlet would like to do a story on what the local academic health center is doing to prepare for a smallpox outbreak. Show them how you operate. Let them know the emergency plans. Show how your staff is being briefed. These topics make great stories for local media, get good coverage, and help establish relationships. The media, in turn, will know who to go to when something happens.

Remember, local media does not mean just the TV station. There are also radio stations and sometimes newspapers. The wire services are a good place to go to. Reuters only operates in major cities, but the Associated Press, for example, is everywhere, and through this wire service, one can reach the entire country and the world with a message.

When practicing emergency scenarios, it is a good idea to include the media. Before September 11, some of the press might have been reluctant to participate, saying they are observers, not participants. That has changed.

People at academic health centers might not immediately anticipate what the media may see as a story, but the media can help them prepare for a story they have in mind. Despite what many people think, the media are not deliberately biased. Most have good intentions. They do consider themselves the fourth estate and feel a duty to inform the public accurately and to make sure that officials do not get out of control.

September 11 has refreshed that feeling and perhaps redirected some media managers and editors from the attitude of media as a business. However, a news organization has to make money, and reporters have to do news on the cheap, the news that people will read, which means entertainment news. This attitude can usually mean making budget cuts by hiring 24-year-olds who are talented, want to work hard, and mean well, but who often do not have the experience or the wisdom to know how to cover a story. This annoys reporters. It probably annoys the public even more, but it is reality, and one needs to know how to deal with it. It is possible that the person doing the first break on a story is a 24-year-old producer at the local television station who does not know anything and will rely strongly on the academic health centers for guidance. Unfortunately, these people do not know that they don't know. They think they know. It helps to get someone a little older and wiser in the local media to be the contact. Experience is important.

The Media: To Tell or Not to Tell?

Another issue concerns what the media should tell and what they should not tell. Some experts have described how nobody would listen to them when they said that bioterrorism was a threat. I personally published list after list of the likely bioterrorist agents. They are also on the CDC's Web pages, yet I am still accused of giving a guidebook to the terrorists. In his book, *Living Terrors*, Dr. Michael Osterholm related scenarios such as anthrax in a ventilation system of the Sears Tower. After the October attacks, he was afraid to quote from his own book because he did not want to give anybody ideas.

It is not the media's job to withhold information. It is their job to disseminate as much information as possible. Obviously, if a life is hanging in the balance, certain information should be withheld. It is easy to decide not to report on enemy troop positions, but there are grayer areas.

How much danger is there that a writer could give a potential terrorist an idea? One of a reporter's worst nightmares is that some hijacker will be arrested carrying in his pocket a story by the reporter who gave him the blueprint for his crime. But this is an unlikely situation, and it is better to err on the side of informing the public. Terrorists use ignorance and fear to their advantage. If the public is informed, people will be calmer. It is a way to defeat the terrorists. Then-Prime Minister Margaret Thatcher said that publicity is the oxygen of a terrorist. But publicity can be oxygen to everybody. Britain has decided to err on the side of making sure people know what the dangers are. They are up front about their security measures, and people there deal with the danger. When there is a bomb in a trash can, people will practically run the police down to get to a store that is right behind the trash can because they do not want their day-to-day lives interrupted by the terrorists. If the nation works to remove any element of fear, it will be the response of the American people as well.

Conclusion

You cannot close Pandora's box once it is open. When an emergency strikes, people need to know what is happening so that they can better distinguish a real threat from hearsay. For their part, health professionals have to be prepared to inform the news media about the latest medical events, so that the press can then disseminate the facts to their various audiences.

Chapter Eleven

Mental Health Services After a Disaster

Betty Pfefferbaum, MD, JD

T he goal of terrorism, evident in the word itself, consists not only of disasters wrought (e.g., destruction and damage of property, injuries and loss of life, grief and sorrow, disruption of commerce and government) but also the sense of fear and intimidation foisted on those who survived. The experience of the Oklahoma City bombing and the mental-health delivery issues that arose shortly after can provide a foundation for understanding the psychological impact of terrorism.

Disaster Victims

There are four classes of disaster victims:

1. Direct victims, the individuals who are physically present at a disaster site.
2. First-responders, the new heroes.
3. Family members of direct victims.
4. Indirect victims, the people residing in a community or a society where a disaster occurs.

The direct victims are presumed to have the most serious psychological consequences, for example, posttraumatic stress disorder (PTSD), which comprises three symptom groups, as follows:

1. Persistent reexperiencing of the traumatic experience that can occur in dreams, memories, flashbacks, et cetera.
2. Numbing and avoidance of reminders of the trauma.
3. Heightened arousal.

However, these three consequences are not the only ones that arise as a result of trauma. Following the Oklahoma City bombing, Carol North, a professor of psychiatry, Washington University School of Medicine in St. Louis, and her colleagues studied a sample of direct victims. Their findings, which are helping mental health providers anticipate some of the results of September 11, indicate that as many as 45 percent of the direct victims developed some psychiatric disorder after the Oklahoma City explosion, including depressive and anxiety disorders. (More than one-third developed PTSD.)

The onset of symptoms was acute and occurred on the day of the blast for many people. Comorbidity was extensive: Over 60 percent of the victims who suffered PTSD had a co-occurring disorder, most commonly, a major depressive disorder, which occurred in over 20 percent of those affected.

First-responders have certainly captured our attention because of their recent work in New York City and earlier in Oklahoma City. Six months after the explosion at the World Trade Center, firefighters were still engaged in the cleanup effort and remained involved for some time thereafter in intensive and terribly enduring work in Oklahoma City. First-responders choose their line of work and are selected for the work that they do, in part, because of their resilience. They are trained and prepared for the crisis response. Although the direct victims' exposure to life-threatening events is typically sudden and unanticipated, the professional rescuers' exposure is likely to last longer. They also commonly have prior experiences with trauma, so their exposure during a rescue or recovery effort builds on previous experiences, which can actually sensitize them for more disastrous or traumatic responses. Finally, their work typically entails a great deal of danger.

The most horrifying aspect of the bombing in Oklahoma City for those who worked as part of the health response was the fact that it targeted children; nineteen were actually killed. Probably the most poignant and compelling work after Oklahoma involved working with the mothers, and in some cases, the grandmothers of these children. Family members suffered a condition known as traumatic grief.

Although a great deal is known about the resolution of grief itself, much less is known about the resolution of traumatic grief, which brings together the symptoms of PTSD (i.e., recurring images and thoughts, arousal, and numbness and detachment) with the more common symptoms of grief. This condition requires careful attention by mental health-care providers to the traumatic aspects of the situation if grief-resolution is to proceed. In addition, the mothers in Oklahoma City had survivor guilt, and some also suffered from "the guilt of modern motherhood." They felt extremely guilty, as most mothers do these days, for having placed their children in day care. Most said they had thought that a day-care center in a Federal building was the safest place they could place their children. A number of the mothers surprisingly talked about having a premonition that something ominous would occur that day, which added another layer of guilt on many of the women.

The indirect victims, those who live in a community or a society where a disaster occurs, have also captured attention. There are indirect victims of all kinds of disasters, even natural disasters. In the case of terrorism, they are as much the intended targets as the direct victims. Indeed, terrorism's randomness is designed to, and certainly does, increase the sense of vulnerability that all of us experience in that kind of situation.

The University of Oklahoma Health Sciences Center has begun to study indirect victims extensively, and investigators have elucidated a number of issues. First, posttraumatic stress disorder symptoms are very common following a disaster. It is difficult, however, to know the implications of this finding. Two studies detailing the posttraumatic stress responses of the general public to September 11, both across the United States and in New York City, identify a vast experience of PTSD symptomology. The symptoms, however, tended to be transient and not to affect functioning, at least not for any significant period of time. Thus, the lasting effect of PTSD is still of some question.

The children in Oklahoma City have figured prominently in the mental-health response in Oklahoma City. Children experience posttraumatic stress symptomology that is basically the same as in adults. However, they have difficulty verbalizing what they feel, and, in some instances, even have trouble conceptualizing what is meant by "numbing" or "detachment." The best way to have access to what they are experiencing is through their play. One of the most common and widespread themes of play among children in Oklahoma City following the bombing was rescue work. It was also evident in New York City.

It is vital that mental health professionals work with the children directly because parents and other adults tend to underestimate the child's distress. Parents have an added burden if they acknowledge their children are in distress. Many children recognize this and try to avoid burdening their parents further by keeping their feelings from the parents. Some children, in the face of disaster, become particularly compliant, at least for a period of months, because they recognize the severity of the new environment.

Factors Affecting Response to Trauma

In terms of risk and resilience related to trauma exposure, studies show that women suffer more PTSD symptoms and are diagnosed more frequently than men, at least in adulthood, but this has not been conclusively determined in children. Age and ethnicity have been harder to study, and it is necessary to keep in mind that ethnicity is accompanied by the confounding factor of socioeconomic status. Exposure to other trauma and preexisting psychiatric conditions are contributing factors to PTSD, as is the degree of exposure to the traumatic experience (typically measured in terms of physical proximity, intensity, and duration of exposure). At least as important is the individual's subjective experience and appraisal of the life threat or danger in the midst of the disaster or terrorist environment.

The study group at the University of Oklahoma has been at the forefront in examining the relationship between media exposure and PTSD symptomology. There is a positive relationship in some samples, particularly in children, but that relationship does not establish cause and effect. Indeed, the thinking is that those individuals who are most traumatized may be more drawn to the media, either to obtain information or to maintain the heightened state of arousal that they are experiencing. However, we have not found the relationship between media exposure and PTSD symptoms to occur across samples. North did not address this link in her study, and we were unable to establish it in the convenient sample of direct victims who were seeking treatment in Oklahoma City.

In addressing mental-health conditions following the U.S. embassy bombings in East Africa, there was no link between media exposure and PTSD symptoms, either in the direct victims or in a group of children who could be considered largely indirect victims. There are a lot of differences between Nairobi and Oklahoma City, including access to media exposure and the volume and intensity of disaster exposure. The issue of media exposure, the positive aspects as well as the traumatizing ones, awaits further investigation.

Individual coping and the recovery environment are also factors in the development of posttraumatic stress reactions. Coping is difficult to study because there are no good measures for it in disaster situations. The recovery environment is even more difficult to study. My several experiences with the professional response to terrorism were in very different communities. In Oklahoma City, only a small number of professionals had been trained or were experienced in disaster work. But Oklahoma City is a small, uncomplicated community where it was relatively easy to train and coordinate the health professionals. Nairobi, on the other hand, is a large community, crowded, and impoverished. The AIDS rate is approximately 15 to 20 percent, and there is virtually no emergency medical infrastructure. These conditions dramatically complicated the rescue and recovery, as well as the ongoing mental-health efforts. In addition, disaster is a way of life in Nairobi. In fact, some of the residents remarked that they were perplexed by our response to this disaster when nobody seemed to care about the many other disasters that they have experienced. This is an issue awaiting the development of good measures and more elaborate study.

Victim Denial

Avoidance, one of the core symptom groups of PTSD, is a crucial issue to keep in mind in a postdisaster environment. It was widely evident in Oklahoma City. For example, a teenage boy ran away after the bombing because his mother had been killed, and he could not bear to go to her funeral. A man whose wife was killed, leaving him with two young children, immediately removed all of her pictures and all remembrances of her from the house. The bombing occurred in the Spring. He reported that as soon as school was out, he would send his children to relatives out of state so that by the time they returned for school in the Fall, they would be over the death of their mother.

Avoidance was also prominent in the therapeutic environment. Many appointments were not kept or were cancelled. These were so many, in fact, that the study team wondered what they were doing wrong. In such situations, of course, outreach is vital.

The trauma of a terrorist incident that is accompanied by widespread and massive casualties does not disappear over time, although it may subside. In Oklahoma City two years after the bombing, the two Federal trials were very traumatizing for the direct victims, some of whom had to testify.

One of the lead witnesses found testifying almost as traumatizing as the bombing experience itself. In general, the September 11 attacks also re-traumatized Oklahoma City victims. In a six-year follow-up study of the Oklahoma City direct victims a month after the attack September 11, the number of people who spontaneously raised the issue of September 11 was startling. Some were housebound for months after September 11; some were hospitalized. Almost seven years after the bombing, a number of highly victimized people who were never in treatment are just now entering treatment.

The Federal Disaster Plan

Disasters are usually local phenomena, and the primary responsibility for disaster mental health lies within the community. It is, therefore, critical to have responders who are themselves members of the community, who know and understand the community, and who will remain in the city after the initial effort has ceased.

However, terrorism raises some questions about looking only at the local approach. First, the geographic boundaries may not be as clear. For example, in a bioterrorist attack that is dispersed through air travel, it is not the local or state government who would respond. Second, terrorism does not target just the direct victims. It is really an attack on the entire nation and the Federal government. Finally, terrorism obviously raises important national security concerns, which are not likely to be left solely to a local or state government, or even to the governments of several states.

The Federal mental health plan, developed out of experiences with natural disasters, guided the work in Oklahoma City. However, the plan needs considerable review as it pertains to situations where there is widespread loss of life and horrific and mutilating injury. The Federal response focuses on normal reactions to disaster, emphasizing services like crisis intervention, support services, triage and referral, and outreach and public education. It is not intended to serve those who suffer serious psychological problems. These victims are supposed to be transferred to more traditional care.

The Federal plan also relies heavily on paraprofessionals who are trained to help in the mental-health education outreach effort following a disaster. The current disaster model, which some mental health professionals have challenged for five years following the Oklahoma City bombing, underestimates the psychological problems of direct victims. It is important to remember that 45 percent of the Oklahoma City victims suffered a psychiatric disorder. If the Federal plan is to rely on paraprofessionals, these people must be well trained in identifying and evaluating PTSD and the risk factors and markers for other psychiatric disorders.

Conclusion

There is a critical need for research and evaluation of what mental-health professionals do and the services they can provide following disasters. A substantial literature, for example, describes the effectiveness of various treatments for PTSD in adults, but there is virtually no literature that describes PTSD treatment in children. There is very little study of the effectiveness of the nation's disaster mental-health approach, which has some serious flaws. In fact, there is a growing challenge to debriefing, one of the most widely practiced and endorsed treatments; in some instances, debriefing not only fails to help people who undergo the process but may even be detrimental to some of them.

We cannot afford to forget what we have learned from these disasters: we must not wait for the next headline to remind us.

Chapter Twelve

The Biotech Effect: New Priorities and Products

Mark Crockett, MD

his paper discusses the feasibility and advisability of establishing a
hospital surveillance network that extends across numerous facilities by building onto existing data-collection software systems.
Rush-Presbyterian-St. Luke's Medical Center, Chicago, serves as the model
for the effort and shows how technology is changing to meet a range of
emergency-preparedness concerns.

Web-Based Hospital Data Systems

Since 1997, IBEX Healthdata Systems has been developing Web-based hospital systems for emergency department surveillance. As seen from
scenarios of bioterror or chemical exposure or simply a large epidemiological event like an outbreak of a virus, the emergency department is one of
the first places where cases and symptoms are going to be seen. In 2000,
therefore, Rush-Presbyterian-St. Luke's Medical Center, one of the premier
hospitals in Chicago, decided to install an emergency department
electronic-data system. Called IBEX Pulsecheck, it keeps track of the patient
from the time he or she is triaged through to the emergency department
disposition. The system records data on patient symptoms and resource
utilization, and tracks them through the department, thus providing a
good idea of the patient's whole hospital stay and building an electronic
medical record.

In the last several months, IBEX has been more focused on bioterrorism and public health surveillance, but the IBEX Pulsecheck project actually began in 2000, when the software company started putting together a network piece to connect all of the hospitals in the Rush system. IBEX operates in hospital systems everywhere from Alaska to Florida. Given its national base, IBEX wanted to install public health surveillance in all these hospitals, but did not have much impetus to do so until recently.

Some experts say that when an organization, in a bolt-on approach, adds technology in a situation, without decreasing labor costs or increasing productivity, it ends up increasing management capital without much benefit. While installing its system at Rush, IBEX focused on conventional goals. The hospital's emergency department is located in a busy, urban area and receives 45,000 patient visits per year. Rush's goals were patient safety, risk management, reduced waiting times, and increased revenue in the emergency department through charge capture.

To increase regulatory compliance and also meet the academic health center's goals, IBEX worked with representatives from the Health Care Financing Administration (HCFA), now the Centers for Medicare and Medicaid Services, to adjust its system to HCFA's regulatory environment. The system went on-line in July 2001 and has been extremely successful.

Expanding into Surveillance

At the same time, the directors of the emergency department at Rush were working to establish a public health surveillance network. IBEX works with a public health surveillance network in forty qualifying hospitals. Qualifying hospitals must be geographically diverse, use a Web-based reporting system, and permit real-time syndromic surveillance and resource utilization measures in the emergency department.

Recently, Chicago had several days of incredible heat in which 300 or 400 people died. Rush's emergency department had been involved in that disaster and the hospital directors were collecting data on it. The natural disaster offered some lessons from both the epidemiological and public health perspectives. Rush is able to collect such data for public health surveillance because it has data-collection systems in place. Although conventional goals, such as better risk-management and increased revenue, drive the data entry, the data set is also useful for public health surveillance.

Data Security and Confidentiality

The data set is limited. IBEX is not asking hospitals to share sensitive data that affect the patients or the hospitals. Instead, IBEX is looking for routine data, such as the patient's age and health complaint. The Rush-Presbyterian-St. Luke's Medical Center is independent of IBEX. IBEX does not hold any of the data collected at Rush or any other hospital affiliated with the network, nor does IBEX collect any data internally. Moreover, IBEX cannot access the data without written permission from the hospital.

IBEX arranges for the various member hospitals in this chain to exercise independent control over where the data go. A governing board decides whether to release the data, transferring control of the dissemination of data from IBEX, a private enterprise, to Rush, a private, nonprofit organization with a public health focus. The data set is maintained on a private network, but the data are transmitted over the Internet. The member hospitals record the patient's chief complaint and age, and general geographic area. The data are encrypted and sent over the Internet on an encrypted line. They represent a real-time report of the patient's presenting complaints and symptoms, and, later, a delayed report will carry additional information, for example, whether the symptoms were determined to result from exposure to anthrax.

Value of the Data

What value can data from public health surveillance at Rush or any other academic health center provide? The system provides epidemiological data for research that can be shared with member hospitals. For example, in the Rush network, a hospital in Alaska receives 5,400 patient visits per year. Hospitals with so few patient visits cannot possibly develop an epidemiological knowledge base to analyze real-time public health surveillance. But by concentrating epidemiological data for research in one place, they are able to share their data with people who can use that information. Similarly, the hospital could look at the surrounding geographic area to determine minimally tolerable levels and, for example, the norm for complaints about shortness of breath.

Responding to Bioterrorism

If an emergency department diagnoses a case of anthrax, the surveillance system warns the central organization collecting the data. The alert triggers an alarm; however, the resource hospital filters the information it has been sharing with public health officials. By starting small and sharing only a limited set of data, false alarms of an epidemic or bioterror can be minimized.

Only by having a good, well-established baseline, can public health data be used to determine whether a disaster is happening. Rush is essentially acting as a resource hospital in the Chicago area to the many hospitals having electronic surveillance systems. It has the alerting system and the data and can provide expertise, for example, on decontamination services. The hospital also has a long-standing affiliation with the local poison control center; the center can quickly make available to Rush most of the antidote concentrations needed in an emergency. Rush can also measure how many hospital beds are available in the surrounding area. If an anthrax attack occurs in Seward, Alaska, Rush has information on the disease and is able to look at specific management techniques for handling the epidemic.

Rush is also producing educational materials that will help hospitals target the areas affected by a bioterror event and manage the people affected. No single emergency department can manage 3,000 cases of disease in a short period of time. The plan is not to build that kind of capacity at one institution or manage 3,000 visits to one particular emergency department. Instead, the resource hospital would print out the real-time data from member hospitals to determine the resources available, redirect patients to different facilities, and manage the resources.

Building on What You Have

The old working model for IBEX is the surveillance system for trauma used in trauma centers and emergency medical services (EMS). Most hospitals are involved in a network of regional trauma centers. Although it is easier to tell whether someone suffered a trauma due to a car accident than to detect an anthrax case, detecting a case of anthrax is not as difficult as building the communication network necessary. Federal sponsorship has been key to the success of trauma centers and EMS activities, which can serve as resources for other health facilities. However, it is easier to do trauma than it is to do infectious disease and chemical exposure that come from a terrorist attack. The IBEX system is emergency-department specific, and is growing in popularity, with some reporting on different segments of illnesses.

In terms of priorities and product, the Rush model has been successful because management has encouraged the entrepreneurial attitude among staff. The emergency department directors felt comfortable exploring additional uses for a system brought in for traditional means.

Academic health centers can do likewise with their data collection systems by encouraging their current vendors to concentrate data collection. IBEX's system is open for accepting data from other hospital systems. Within their own systems, academic health centers ought to be encouraging other health care facilities to share data, abiding by the tenet that privacy and security must be maintained. Today, many vendors want to get involved in public health surveillance and would be happy to work with academic health centers.

Conclusion

A data collection network installed to meet traditional goals can produce extraordinary results. Hospitals do not have to go beyond their current needs to develop helpful products. Academic health centers may already be collecting the kinds of data necessary for public health surveillance. Many already have access to and control over the resources necessary to successfully build progressive educational and analytical systems.

In the current environment, the old adage of chance favoring the prepared mind is something that health care entities can apply with success to their own situations.

/